THE MILFORD SERIES

Popular Writers of Today

VOLUME ONE

Robert A. Heinlein
Stranger in His Own Land

Second Edition

George Edgar Slusser

R. REGINALD

THE **Borgo Press**

SAN BERNARDINO, CALIFORNIA

MCMLXXVII

to Hatch
"Mars with its reddish glow . . ."

Library of Congress Cataloging in Publication Data:

Slusser, George Edgar.
    Robert A. Heinlein: stranger in his own land.

    (Popular Writers of Today; v.1) (The Milford Series)
    Bibliography: p.
    1.   Heinlein, Robert Anson, 1907-   —Criticism and in-
terpretation.
PS3515.E288Z87 1977   813'.5'4   77-5657
ISBN 0-89370-210-2

R. Reginald, The Borgo Press is a wholly-owned subsidiary of
Lynwyck Realty and Investment Company, Inc., P.O. Box 2845,
San Bernardino, CA 92406.

First Edition———April, 1976
Second Edition———July, 1977

INTRODUCTION

This study examines a unique mode of didactic writing in the later fiction of Robert A. Heinlein. It describes a process. More and more in his recent novels, Heinlein manipulates the literary conventions he adopts to highly personal ends. The adventure novel becomes a parable, its universal language of action the vehicle for a very private view of the world. The novel of formation, satire and the moral character—Heinlein deploys this venerable machinery to the ultimate purpose of elevating self as ideal standard. The first edition of this book sought to elucidate these transformations. Here I wish to restate my premises.

Heinlein is not a writer of psychological fiction. Nor is he, at the outset, a writer of fiction of ideas. True, there has always been a strong didactic tendency in his work. Most of his novels of the '40s and '50s, however, are classic tales of adventure. Here, by convention, a hero grows as the result of his actions: his character is shaped as events confront him and choices are made. To this extent, Heinlein's early fiction is interested in character development.

It is this conventional pattern that Heinlein first "subverts." *Starship Troopers* (1959) is usually seen as the turning point. Here is a new novel: what might have been the old adventure hero turns out to be a new, exemplary figure. *Troopers* is not, however, the beginning. In two apparently orthodox novels of 1956, *Time for the Stars* and *Double Star*, a curious transformation of the adventure pattern is already well underway. These are interesting hybrids: they begin as action stories, only to end as illustrative or cautionary tales. Just how incompatible these two modes can be is made evident here. The reader is drawn into one world, with its insecurity of linear action and promise of growth through individual achievement. Then, all at once, a rapid series of shifts hurls him into another world: a preordained design is revealed and gradually an elaborate system of guidance becomes clear. The hero did not grow, because he did not really make his own choices—they were made for him. He can only recognize what he was all along; in doing so, he accepts his exemplary destiny. Heinlein's problem in these novels is getting from one world to the other. To do so, he develops an elaborate art of ellipsis.

But why call these novels "subverted"? Is it not simply a matter of an awkward transition, a writer turning from adventure stories to didactic forms? There is still a strange awareness here of contending literary patterns. Heinlein seems to play a game with his reader, methodically emptying one set of forms, yet retaining this hollow framework in order to mask other, subliminal activities. In these two tales, the heroic pattern, though devitalized, lingers on. The shade of the old hero who will not exist confers a kind of specious authority on his emergent double—the man who did not choose but was chosen. A like subversion is true of the world view as well. Heinlein's early adventure novels project a clear vision of man: through the tenacious struggle of individuals, he will progress as a whole, conquering the stars. These nascent exemplary novels do not codify this cosmic work ethic so much as undercut it. A facade remains—characters will expound the virtues of action. But the facts belie this. Beneath the surface, a contrary dynamic begins to operate, one shaped by some gloomier current, with definite Calvinistic overtones. More and more, individual deeds are not enough; destiny becomes purely a matter of election. Even in the early *Time for the Stars*, this is already clear. Of the two twins, one is apparently more suited for action and adventure, the other less. But, as things work out, the latter is taken—reluctantly he must act out the epic pattern. We learn, however, in the end, that he was the right one after all. His introspective nature may make him less effectual as a hero, but a hero is not wanted. Willed action, in general, proves of little use. Instead, Heinlein uses what he calls "serendipity"— you dig for worms, and strike gold. As it turns out, the withdrawn Tom is more valuable to this collective effort. All is guided for the best by Heinlein's secular providence.

Increasingly in the later novels, the traditional center of the adventure story—reasoned and willed deeds—is emptied and elided. We are left with something like the Emersonian polarity of point and circumference: the chosen hero, and the elite group with which he directly interacts. Indeed we only appear, in a work like *Time for the Stars*, to abandon the individual for some wider, collective vision. If anything, Heinlein's old juvenile hero was more basically "democractic": frequently a small-town nobody is propelled into a heroic situation, and rises to the challenge. The protagonists of these "subverted" novels may be reluctant, but they are anything but Everyman. The timorous actor Smythe, in *Double Star*, finds he can fill the shoes of the political leader Bonforte. But he can do so because, beneath all surface disparity, there is one basic affinity: he holds the same "enlightened" view of things: he was one of the elite all along.

Heinlein's first overtly philosophical novel, *Stranger in a Strange Land* (1961), goes further yet. In *Double Star*, the circumference is a social organization, a secret cabal of superior beings. And in *Starship Troopers*, we have those fabled "few good men." In *Stranger*, however, it is less Smith's disciples, or even his "religion," than Smith the man. Here the institution is clearly his lengthened shadow. Heinlein goes through an elaborate ritual of formation, produces his "representative" man, only to drop the mask suddenly—Smith is superman. The polar configuration alters significantly. Now, to Smith's circumferential powers, the supremely self-reliant Harshaw provides the point. In this novel, Heinlein may add a comic heaven to show that the real God is man. But clearly not just any man is God. Indeed, his two central figures are the elite of the elect.

Stranger offers even more profound changes. Where the basic rhythm before was the chosen man's relation with some objective totality, now self and totality tend to become one. Harshaw and Smith are only apparently complimentaries— age and youth. In dialogue, they are more mirror images than anything else: opposing ideas are not debated so much as the same view (in various disguises) is restated and refined. Dialogue, like adventure before it, has become an empty form as well.

This telescoping of center and circumference marks Heinlein's other big novel of the decade, *I Will Fear No Evil*, and reaches an extreme point in his latest, hugest creation, *Time Enough for Love* (1973). In this incredible fresco, all actors and interlocutors can be reduced to one center—Lazarus Long. Old or young, male or female, parent or child—all are, quite literally, his incarnations. In the world of this consummate Narcissus, all action becomes monodrama, all discourse monologue. Ironically, the novel is Heinlein's most multifacted structure: a full-blown *roman-a-tiroirs*. Yet, much more radically even than in *Stranger*, all interplay of situations and ideas is denied, all diversity cancelled in the oscillation of poles now completely become identical. Here (or till Heinlein writes another novel), the process of "subversion" has reached an end. Obviously, far more is at stake here than a switch of genre, a writer trading his juvenile epic for more "mature" didactic forms. Out of Heinlein's persistant fascination with election, with the transcendental polarity, has come first a vision of god as man, then of man as god: contraction to the point, and expansion out from it. Behind Lazarus too, perhaps, by analogy, stands the writer himself as god. Heinlein first absorbed the traditional forms, now he reels them out in virtuoso profusion. But what before was a literary game has now, apparently, become an obsession.

This study was taken to task for not seeing that Heinlein's "approach to human nature" owes its greatest debt to the 18th century. Not only does this misconstrue my argument; it is simply not true. Increasingly, it is true, Heinlein uses forms he seems to have borrowed from 18th century literature: part of *Stranger* is a *Bildungsroman* of the edifying type; and *Time* is a complex "life," a work full of the illustrative tales and discourse current during the Enlightenment. Yet the world view that informs these patterns is anything but 18th century. In his vision of man, Heinlein is heir rather to a tenacious form of American Romanticism. We cannot possibly imagine him, with Pope, calling man "the glory, jest and riddle of the world"—a fascinating creature, but still a mean. Heinlein works rather on the peculiarly American Romantic extremes—at once parochial and universal—of Emerson's self-reliance and transcendental-ism, of Whitman's conservative nationalism and rhapsodic faith in technological progress.

Moreover, in his conception of the artist's task—as we see it in his approach to literary creation—Heinlein is surprisingly "modern" in the Swiftian sense of the word. In his latest novels, we recognize the famous spider. Traditional forms—in-cluding, ironically, those of the 18th century moralists and satirists themselves—are absorbed by the all-devouring writer, and then spun out again in the familiar maze-like structures. In this light, Heinlein's progress is quite predictable: first he seeks to universalize his private philosophy; when this proves too modest an ambition, he strives to universalize himself. Indeed, when Heinlein gives his human paragon Lazarus Long his own Missouri boyhood, he commits a supreme act of literary narcissism.

Surely this is "modernism" again run wild, and in need of some corrective. It is impossible to hide this vision of things by saying (as the fan magazines have tended to do) that Hein-lein's later novels are simply careless patchworks, slapped together by a tired old writer from scraps in his drawer, and thus can be disregarded. Such a view is not only hopelessly nostalgic; it is patently false. Heinlein obviously intends a work like *Time Enough For Love* to be the keystone of his opus, his literary *summum*. Nor should we be misled by a formalism that would study these works as "objects," *in vitro*. To such critics, it is irrelevant that Heinlein gives Lazarus his own bio-graphy: the characters are not the author. But if Heinlein is a master of *persona*, it is surely not in the usual sense. His is hardly the Swiftian interest in multiple perspectives, the ironic reduction of extremes to some acceptable human mean. Hein-lein's creative rhythm, rather, flees the middle, undulating be-tween extremes. If we accept this paradigm, it is easy to find one man talking out of all forms and all mouths.

Certainly, larger issues are raised here. Particularly in-triguing is the degree to which Heinlein is conscious of what he is doing. Surely (the argument goes) no writer would consciously develop, at these impossible lengths, such elaborately solipsistic structures. There has to be a point where the individual creative consciousness loses control, where some larger cultural pattern or myth takes over. The temptation is to evoke abstractions like the "American mind." This study, however, is not primarily interested in metaphysics or sociology. Its focus holds at that point where certain broader patterns (be they American, Romantic, or mythic) interact with the various literary conventions Heinlein the writer chooses to use.

Nor, in the same sense, is this a "liberal" attack on a "conservative" writer. It is true that Heinlein's later novels have been misunderstood—disastrously at times. People supposedly on the "left" were claiming them for their camp, where even by the wildest stretch of the imagination they do not belong. This study tries to explain Heinlein's "philosophy" as it goes— it is impossible not to react to its more reprehensible aspects. What is interesting, however, is not that Heinlein is conservative, but that his conservatism taps at many points what seem to be the roots of national myth. The configurations of his latest novels may represent an extreme—and frightening—development of what is a constant and deep current in American life and letters.

This is not meant, however, to be a portrait in literary madness. My essay seeks to bring to light patterns in Heinlein's fiction below the level of themes, conventions, doctrines, and see how these central dynamics (which belong, if anything, to the realm of cultural myth) generate formal structures. Heinlein's world view, though professedly secular and scientific, is actually impregnated with the patterns of native Calvinism. In fact, many of the 'contradictions' critics have seen in Heinlein's attitude and pronouncements can be reduced to this common base. The glories and anxieties of Heinlein's brand of predestination not only shapes his ideas, but also guides his structural choices as well.

TWINS AND DOUBLES

At first glance, *Time for the Stars* and *Double Star* may seem to be ordinary Heinlein novels—the former a typical "juvenile" adventure among the stars, the latter an exercise in the sort of political intrigue that forms the nucleus of his "adult" tales of the '40s and '50s. Actually, their structure is quite different. Critics have noticed, in Heinlein, a general tendency toward fast starts and quagmire middles. Here, however, change of pace has become something more radical—there is a sense of rupture, of disconnected halves. Both works begin as traditional adventure tales and end as openly exemplary portraits. In between, there is less transition than hiatus. What does this signify?

It might appear, at first, that Heinlein is striving to create some new (and modern) form of didactic fiction. Traditionally, literature of this sort sets the individual case in a general frame, subsuming it under an unassailable law. The relationship of parts, then, is fundamentally static. But if Heinlein has no such universally acknowledged canons to draw upon, must he not derive his general statement from some particular set of actions? The pattern in Heinlein is dynamic and linear. The initial promise of action is a promise that values will be tested, not just arbitrarily asserted; individual conflict should in some way justify the exemplary conclusions ultimately drawn from it. These two novels, however, follow no such development. At the outset, there is no hint we are dealing with anything even remotely illustrative: we plunge feet-first into the concrete world of action. Then, without warning, come a series of ironic manipulations. One by one, traditional expectations are sapped and the conventions of heroic adventure "subverted." In the final pages, the heroic pattern has become hollow. We are at a loss to explain why Heinlein does this. Indeed, the "philosophy" his figures finally enunciate is still, if stated in general terms, one of action and struggle. And yet, paradoxically, it issues forth from a process of ellipsis that systematically undercuts the very moments of individual action that lend credence to such a moral.

These two novels are direct ancestors of *Starship Troopers*. Many critics view that work as one where Heinlein takes his old hard-boiled scrapper, and openly, belligerently glorifies him: as the sermon grows, the action shrinks. My view is contrary. Dominated by ellipsis, the structure of these novels must negate all possibility of individual action. In the traditional heroic novel (and Heinlein has written these), an individual chooses, then accomplishes his chosen ends through willed deeds. Now, as this process is suspended, men are elected, and lifted to positions of eminence irrespective of their actions or heroic merit. Structual rhythms are at odds with the message, a predestined aristocracy incompatible with more democratic exhortations to mankind in general. The deeper significance of Heinlein's emerging didactic tale is found in this disparity.

By its very title, *Time for the Stars* creates familiar expectations: adventure in space, conflict and resolutions. It is the story of twin brothers, Tom and Pat, who possess the rare ability to communicate telepathically. Because of their skill, one will be chosen to join the crew of the torchship *Lewis and Clark*: an overcrowded Earth is seeking new worlds to colonize. Since thought travels faster even than light, the telepathic twins will insure communication between ship and Earth. In spite of Pat's apparently stronger personality, chance designates Tom, and he goes. As the ship approaches the speed of light, Pat grows old; first his daughter, and then his grand-daughter replace him as the telepathic link. The vessel makes two landings on new worlds. There is the usual attack by hostile aliens; this is followed by the threat of mutiny aboard ship. In the nick of time, however, the survivors are saved from disaster. Against all hope and logic, a new space drive is invented. It brings Tom home for an unexpected final reunion with his aged twin.

Thus summarized, the story seems banal enough. For Heinlein, however, the novel is unusual in its narrative emphasis. Not only is it about a hero with an inferiority complex; it is told by him as well. Many of Heinlein's juvenile heroes are apparent underdogs in one manner or another. Once forced into action, they discover hidden powers, acquitting themselves admirably. From the outset, Tom is unusually introspective. And because he tells the tale, he has free rein to indulge in self-examination. As he does so, the usual thrust of the juvenile action novel—out to the stars—is relocated inside his mind. What seems to be shaping up is a psychodrama. If Tom is to be a hero at all, his mode of heroism will be subjective, not objective, self-domination through contemplation, rather than fulfillment of self in action. Yet the machinery of the action plot is inexorable—and it moves in the opposite direction: the ship must take off, the twins must be separated. Whatever the psychological struggles between these two, the laws of Einsteinian physics alone will ultimately resolve them. Heinlein keeps his two minds in contact as long as possible—almost two-thirds of the novel drags by till we get to the promised action in the stars. It is not some inner process of selfmastery that finally frees Tom from his personal traumas, and allows him to give his attention to events going on around him. It is the purely external fact of the time lag. Indeed, the twins' drama is destined to be resolved by the very course of events which originally heightened it: *Project Lebensraum*.

Once the ship is launched, we gradually realize that the subject of the book is not Tom and Pat, but the Project itself. The ship is a microcosm, a floating laboratory, full of scientists studying phenomena apparently of no immediate use to this particular voyage. In this perspective, Tom's personal problems become just one more case of time-lag stress. Conveniently, the Foundation has provided a psychologist in residence, who observes, analyzes and prescribes therapy. In terms of the collective effort, individuals have become valuable sources of data. At one point, Tom even comes to refer to himself and his fellows as "spare parts." And in a sense, this is what all beings aboard have become—parts, expendable if necessary, of a complex human machine.

We wait a long time for Tom's inner problems to be resolved.

And when they finally are, he does not, as we might expect, move from introspection to the role of classic hero. Initially, the narrative focus is inward: Tom talks almost exclusively about himself. Heinlein must free him so that he can both participate in external events, and yet recount them. The change occurs suddenly rather than gradually. An odd ellipsis places this voice on a very different level. Halfway through the novel, Heinlein makes a surprising revelation: we have not been listening to Tom at all, we have been reading his diary. Everything in the first part of the book is not the immediately-experienced reality it first appeared to be: Tom has been looking at himself in the same way the ship's scientists examine their specimens. This diary, in fact, is the therapy the psychologist had prescribed, and we are meant to assume that the very act of writing it has freed Tom from his neuroses. Time in the novel plays strange tricks on the characters, so why should it not on the readers as well? The focus on a hero is only an illusion. As we read of Tom's struggles, they are already past. The diary continues beyond this point of revelation. But where Tom had once contemplated himself from the safe distance of modern psychology, now he watches the action more or less from the periphery as well. His account of the ensuing adventures of the *Lewis and Clark* reads more like a logbook than anything else. Tom has become the voice of the ship, the historian of a microcosmic community embarked on a special quest.

Oddly, as Tom's voice becomes that of the community, the adventures that traditionally should have been his alone become collective endeavors: we are meant to see the ship and crew as the only true hero now. The explorers land on two planets: one turns out to be paradise, the other a hellish nightmare. Clearly, their adventure is intended to be as exemplary as Tom's psychodrama turned out to be. Mankind too, just like the individual, is groping in the dark. Man thinks he will like paradise, but the interlude on this planet proves that unending bliss can be tiring: man must have challenge and change. On the other hand, the terrible destruction experienced on the ironically misnamed Elysia demonstrates mankind's propensity to error, his relative helplessness against the forces of chaos. In these actions, Tom, unlike the traditional hero, plays only an ancillary role. Because of his value as telepath, he is forbidden to leave the ship. On Constance, he sets foot on solid ground only after the testing has been completed and the planet declared safe. And in the battle with the amphibians of Elysia, he must sit on the sidelines and watch his comrades he slaughtered. His "time for the stars," it seems, is just more time to fret and to watch.

Those who survive Elysia now face the seemingly impossible task of returning home alive. Under this stress, it appears, even the collective center cannot hold. Here Heinlein borrows an idea from an earlier juvenile, *Starman Jones* (1953), and gives Tom one last heroic possibility: where authority is blind to the general good, the individual who sees it must revolt. As with Jones, Tom becomes a figure of influence through sheer attrition: he is the only functioning telepath left, hence the only one who stands a chance of pulling the ship through. In *Starman Jones*, however, the hero revolts, triumphs, and in so doing proves himself as an individual. Tom on the other hand neither succeeds nor fails—anticlimactically, he gives in to the teachings of Uncle Steve, his now-dead mentor. Steve was a military man who believed that the Captain is always right, no matter what. Here is another exemplum wrung from a subverted convention. Mutiny and internal strife are worse evils than stupidity: man is already weak enough, and to divide forces can only make him weaker. Tom learns to bend his individual urgings to the common weal.

Indeed, our faith in teamwork will be rewarded in the end, in a way both surprising and unforeseeable. The logic of the situation hits us like a burst of inspiration. All throughout the voyage, the scientists on board have pursued their individual manias, sending their findings back to Earth routinely, with no specific goal in mind. Here is "pure" research at its most ideal. Due to relativity, however, engineers at home have had many years to experiment and find applications. One of these is a revolutionary new space drive: "null-field" generators render the old mode of travel, measured in light-years, "irrelevant."

A rescue party meets the ship and brings our explorers home. This is what Heinlein calls "serendipity."

And yet, if this novel extols collective effort, it does so in a very odd way. The scientists of the *Lewis and Clark* form a strange community. Each follows his own passion, to the exclusion of others, and in open scorn of any master plan. Even group heroism is undermined. Not only does purposive individual action go astray, but all attempts to impose rational control on the process of human evolution seem futile as well. Action is reduced to mere motive force: it is better to move than stand still. But the rest is in the hands of "serendipity." This, however, is more than just good luck. In the larger evolutionary sweep of this novel, its impact is that of providence itself. Moreover, it appears with inexplicable rapidity, coming unbidden and unearned, almost like some secular form of grace. Einsteinian law seems insurmountable. But in a flash, man leaps from the agonizing question: 'will there ever be time for the stars?' to the rousing call for victory: 'now it's time for the stars!' Both are in the title. Clearly, though, this kernel is not cracked by willed action; it opens when it is ready.

One may ask why mankind, capable of so little on its own, is chosen for this glorious destiny among the stars. Even more, one wonders why some are chosen, and others are not. Why Tom, and not Pat, for instance? The unlikely one from the start, Tom never does achieve heroic stature through his deeds. Naturally, we later learn that Pat was no hero either; if anything he was even less emotionally stable than his brother. What is more, we see that old-fashioned heroism is not wanted here after all. The ways of destiny are wonderful, if inscrutable. And why these particular scientists? Heinlein purposely gives them plain, humble exteriors. Dr. Babcock is a great physicist, yet looks and talks "like a lumberjack." Here are aristocrats neither by birth, nor by any conventional sign. Nor by actions either, for they, like Tom, also dig for worms, working in the dark. To some, Heinlein seems an apostle of scientific rationalism, to others a proponent of Social Darwinism, the survival of the fittest. Both are masks. Beneath lies quite a contrary current. Already functioning here is a mysterious process of election, that separates wheat from chaff in ways inexplicable to moralist and logician alike.

In a book whose structure is dominated by ellipsis, it is interesting that the epilogue re-enacts the situation of that archetypal elided life, Rip Van Winkle. Tom and his fellow pioneers return to Earth to find that things have evolved beyond them. Rip was offered the perfect solution to the adult world of choice and individual struggle: he slept through these years. When he returns, time alone has solved his marital problems. The war is over; as a curiosity, he becomes a sort of hero without having earned it. Increasingly, Heinlein's protagonists will follow this pattern of development. Rip, of course, pays for his good fortune—his youth is gone. Heinlein, however, improves on his model. Tom is out of phase with this brave new world; yet as he "slept," he was unwittingly helping all the while to bring it into being. And his Einsteinian sleep has favored him: he is still young. Heinlein confronts his new Rip with the aged twin Pat. Of the two identical beings, one was chosen, the other not. In this final confrontation, the awful reality of election leaps physically before our eyes.

Double Star, although a similar example of the subversion of convention, has a somewhat different thrust. If its hero, Lorenzo Smythe, is also a "spare part," he is handled in a different manner. This novel begins as a fast-paced adventure, only to bog down as Smythe, in the hands of various mentors and teachers, comes face to face with himself. First he must prove to himself that he can impersonate a political leader on the stage of life. He discovers his identity in the process, only to be called upon to renounce it. The leader dies, and now he must *become* that person for good. In *Time for the Stars*, Tom's problems were solved by destiny and luck. Here the leap from individual to exemplary man, apparently, involves choice, self-control, and conscious acceptance. Heinlein has turned the process of subversion around, using it more skillfully. The result is a unified novel, and also one which is, far more consciously, a piece of subterfuge.

In its opening pages, *Double Star* is a conventional spy thriller. Things move so swiftly that the subsequent shift in perspective is a letdown. Smythe is a hero in the traditional mold: we have the vainglorious but impecunious actor, master of stage fustian, but timorous and quite naive in real life. He is the typical cautious innocent. Smythe blunders into danger without being aware of the situation, and is manipulated by professionals to their own ends. The incongruity between Lorenzo's verbal bravado and real-life cowardice is exploited to comic effect: he is drawn into a shoot-out, obliged to butcher and dispose of three humans and one Martian. In all of this, he is a most reluctant participant; at one point, he even tries to duck out of the game through the bathroom window.

To sustain this pace, the novel should lead Lorenzo from one event to another until, in spite of himself, he accidentally stumbles on the heart of the mystery. But this is not what happens. Mystery and conspiracy are overwhelmed by other preoccupations. Lorenzo is given a job to do: he must stand-in for the kidnapped leader Bonforte, whom he resembles. The focus now shifts to the intricate mechanics of this task. Tom is given a mentor, Uncle Steve, to help him assume his proper role in the collective process. Lorenzo has Dak Broadbent. In *Time for the Stars*, however, the multiple centers of interest, the complexity of the social organism itself, separate Steve from Tom for long periods. Tom needs guidance often, and the recurring possibilities for action draw him back again and again to the heroic temptation. But Steve too has his role. Battle duty calls him away from his charge; he is killed. Awkwardly, Heinlein is forced to resurrect Steve's ghost (in the form of sage advice) in order to tame Tom's rebellion against the foolish Captain.

The mentor figure is more skillfully handled in *Double Star*. Present from the very first page, Dak maneuvers his unwilling pupil through some tight scrapes, spirits him away to a safe location, and then stays on to direct his education. Whenever Lorenzo has a moment of doubt, Dak pops in to incite or advise. With Dak too, appearances are most deceiving: this future

James Bond turns out to be the Hon. Darius K. Broadbent, Ph.D. in physics, and a renowned space-poet (under a pseudonym of course). Like the plain-speaking scientists of *Time for the Stars*, he is one of Heinlein's new aristocrats. Dak, however, transcends "serendipity". Now the chosen one has become, in turn, an instrument in the process of election. From the beginning, mentors are ubiquituous in Heinlein's novels. As the adventure convention dictates, they are merely strong men. The emphasis is still on deeds. Dak however, though a man of action, is even more a guide, the means of effecting a kingdom of the elect on earth. Significantly, it is he who chooses Lorenzo, and then leads him by the hand to that moment when he too realizes that he belongs to the select company.

The mystery plot of the opening pages hardly requires that the hero become self-conscious or wiser. On the contrary, this would undercut the comic effects derived from his naive bumblings. Heinlein, however, turns this convention inside out. He sequesters Lorenzo. Then he leads him through a series of internal crises to an ultimate moment of decision. To do so, he subverts the tale of intrigue, thwarting our expectations at each step. The spy story calls for a *femme fatale* to lead the hero astray. Heinlein gives us the over-emotional Penny. She had secretly loved her former boss Bonforte, and thus resents Smythe's imposture. At any moment she may break down, giving the whole thing away. As with Tom's inferiority complex, this potential personal crisis is dangled before us, yet never allowed to develop. Again a psychologist hovers in the wings. But even he, it turns out, is not needed. Things once more are blunted by the natural course of time, and in wondrous ways. As Lorenzo gets better at impersonating Bonforte, Penny falls for him as well. Such is the power of art that they even get married at the end of the book. This solution may seem dangerously vicarious: on each side we are once removed from reality. In this novel, however, what seems fantasy opens onto a higher reality, a predetermined harmony, where Lorenzo does become Bonforte, and where Penny marries the right man after all.

The characters in this book are no more individuals than in *Time for the Stars*. We have only a different category of types: there it was scientific man, here political man. The counterpart of the scientist-technician is the political organizer: Rog Clifton is a doer, not a talker, a man who gets things done. There are more egregious stereotypes. The kind and saintly Uncle Alfred of *Time for the Stars* has as counterpart here another gentle darkie, the faithful errand boy Jimmie Washington. Women in both novels are either helpless, whining creatures, or prudes—discardables. At their best, women and Blacks are fit to be servants and adulators of the elect, no more.

Types are to be expected in the novel of intrigue. But something else is not: the absence of aggressive, absolute evil. The convention calls for sharp delineation between the good and bad guys. The thrust of the action is, invariably, to uncover and smash the unprincipled opposing organization. The opponents in *Double Star*, however, are curiously ineffectual. There is a problem of evil in Heinlein, but it is of a most unusual sort.

Two sources of potential evil exist here—villians and traitors, the evil without and that within. Significantly, this outer enemy remains unseen, faceless throughout. Its nature is precisely circumscribed. In Heinlein's novels, men encounter obstacles and opposition, but never gratuitous evil. Many men are lost on hostile Elysia. But if there is "evil" here, it is more man's than anything else. In misnaming the planet, he had presumed the existence of a better place, substituting his wishes for reality. The word "sin" fits better here—his is the error of intellectual pride. The Humanist Party (Bonforte's kidnappers) is short-sighted, xenophobic, afraid of the unknown. They too err in arrogantly dictating boundaries to man's capabilities and destiny. Taking an action that seems infallibly favorable to their cause, they ironically bring about the opposite end together with their downfall: the Expansionists win. Moreover, a new rejuvenated "Bonforte" is now at their head.

The presence of the traitor illustrates just how widespread this primal error is. Like his villains, Heinlein's betrayers are not agents of absolute evil either. In *Time for the Stars*, there are two potential enemies within—Pat and Capatin Urquart. But neither is diabolical. They are simply narrow-minded and proud. The same is true for Bill Corpsman in *Double Star*. One of the Expansionist cadre, he denounces Lorenzo's impersonation publicly at a press conference. Bill has reasons for his treachery: he is jealous of Lorenzo, and he is the only one of the group without a constituency. We see his motives, and even sympathize. Yet we also despair. These are personal failings, to be sure. But how correctible and eradicable are they? Behind them all lies the tenacious fault of pride. Ironically, although this is a tale of intrigue, Smythe apparently has little to fear from without. Bill's action is proof of this. His betrayal should be devastating; actually, it is harmless. Lorenzo keeps cool, Rog manipulates behind the scenes, and Bill ends up making a fool of himself. His evil is shown to be stupidity and weakness. What is more, it is ineffectual. Something like "serendipity" is at play again, working for Lorenzo and against Bill. Ultimately the offender tells why he did it: pathetically, he only wanted to be closer to Lorenzo. More than power, the man's aura drew him. But does this mean that, if we understand the motives of men like Bill, we can correct and reclaim them? The implication is quite the contrary. Bill Corpsman (even the name is ironic) only seemed part of the inner circle; in reality, he was always an outsider. That is why he had no constituency. Once his menace is pushed aside, he is simply dropped and forgotten. Not one of the elect, he was destined to go astray; reprobate, he is unredeemable. Heinlein makes this point: the real enemy is not a party or cabal, but a general human disposition. If Lorenzo is safe from external danger, what of this danger within? Heinlein would make it appear that his real struggle is with pride and selfishness. The climax of this psychodrama seems to come when he must choose between himself and a higher destiny—to be or not to be Bonforte. But like the spy plot, this too is empty form. The choice was made long before—and not by Lorenzo. He was picked, provided sanctuary, aided by teachers and all the marvels of science, and led by the hand to his final moment of "recognition." He is Bonforte's double in more ways than just physical resemblance. As we shall see, there are deeper, elective affinities.

The initial action plot never completely disappears. Ripples of intrigue surface periodically throughout the book. The possibility of crisis is, however, always disarmed, and the thrust of the action redirected in a curious manner. Lorenzo's first ordeal, for instance, is to stand in for Bonforte during the "adoption" ceremony at the Martian nest. Failure to appear would not only be a fatal breach of etiquette—a setback for the Expansionist policy—but would also reveal Bonforte's abduction, precipitate new elections, and probably sweep his party from power. One would expect the other side to stop Lorenzo at all costs. Their efforts, however, are amateurish and feeble, all too easily thwarted. The real problem, we discover, comes from within: the smell of Martians nauseates Smythe. Crisis builds in the actor's mind. But this too is artificial. At the last minute, the psychiatrist comes to the rescue. The solution is (as always in Heinlein) ingenious and yet so simple: he conditions the hero to associate Martian's with the smell of Penny's perfume. What could have been torture becomes perfect bliss.

Lorenzo's subsequent mental tribulations are staged with similar artificiality. Instead of action, we have titillation. Bonforte is finally rescued. The hero sighs with relief, only to learn that his brain has been paralyzed with drugs—the show must go on. Doctors have hopes the drugs will wear off. But each time Smythe sees light at the end of the tunnel, Bonforte has another relapse. Supposedly we are building to the peak: the leader dies (in most timely fashion) after seeing himself and party re-elected for a new term. Lorenzo's earlier struggles were of a different order: he must take the leap alone. To remain Bonforte is to give up Smythe, to relinquish his being. The quandary is potentially devastating to his mind. At this point, Heinlein resorts to ellipsis.

As with *Time for the Stars*, the figure of ellipsis dominates *Double Star*. Instead of telling us what happened at the Martian adoption ceremony, for example, Heinlein gives a row of asterisks: it is improper for an initiate to reveal such secrets.

Once Lorenzo had put his own house in order, of course, the rest was irrelevant. But now it looks as if the book will end with his house more out of order than ever. Suddenly though, on the last page, we learn that what we have been reading is really an account Smythe wrote twenty-five years earlier to "straighten out my own confusion". It is Rip Van Winkle again. We do not see the man heal himself, but must assume he has. As we read, he wrote; in this ingenious *stretto* exercise, both arrive at the same point together. Conspicuously, however, conscious action is replaced by passive submission to the fortunate workings of time. For the reader, this is elided—in a flash, Lorenzo is cured. In its ending, the book re-enacts the stroke of grace.

On the surface, a novel of intrigue has been cleverly "subverted", and turned into a didactic vehicle. The message seems to be Heinlein's old "philosophy" of man: his duty is to strive and go forward; to do so, he must avoid stupid limitations—superstition and xenophobia. Lorenzo appears to grow: the man who in the beginning could not bear the physical presence of a Martian becomes, in the end, champion of union between earthmen and the non-human peoples of the Solar System. But should we see in this fairy-tale ending a destiny open to all mankind? Lorenzo does grow through heroic effort, either of body or of mind; he is lifted to eminence. Nor can we forget that he and Bonforte are doubles. On the outside, of course, they seem very different men—it seems impossible the twain can meet. But here again is revelation. However disparate the language, their views of life turn out to be the same. Bonforte has written learned tomes; Lorenzo says it simply: "Always take sides!"; "The show must go on!"

Again this rousing cry masks a deeper—and far less optimistic—pattern of meaning. The two heroes are doubles in a more fundamental sense. As the actor embraces the politician's view of things, he discovers in a flash it was his all along. When he first meets the great man, Lorenzo experiences the shock of grace: "I felt that warm, almost holy shock one feels when first coming into sight of the great statue of Abraham Lincoln." In his final comment on his impersonation, Smythe cites Voltaire:

"If Satan should ever replace God, he would find it necessary to assume the same attributes of divinity". Satan, however, is not Everyman. One prince replaces another; we are dealing with beings in the divine circle of the elect. Once more, the title of novel holds the key. On one level, the word "star" points to man's glorious destiny. On a deeper plane, though, it tells us who will lead mankind on such a quest: the "stars", these aristocrats by election.

Behind Heinlein's pattern of fortunate paradoxes a mode of providence is at work—an operation as partial as it is inexplicable. Lorenzo must give up his very being, but is not broken. In astounding fashion, rather than losing self, he gains it in becoming the other, for both are same. Similarly, the world gains with the death of Bonforte. The drugs forced on him had aged him prematurely. When Lorenzo takes his place, even devouring time is cheated. In his disguise, we have a younger man in an old mask. Time will stand still as he grows into his role.

Obviously, these two novels of 1956 intend to present exemplary lives. Their didactic conclusions seem to evolve out of a base of heroic struggle. Heinlein's earlier heroes fought and won. Is he not now seeking to generalize, to draw a moral from the heroic process? Actually, both the objective and subjective modes of action are "subverted" here, emptied of meaning and power to shape. Whether Heinlein is totally conscious of what he does in these books is questionable. The result nonetheless is obvious. On the surface, the novel becomes a pulpit: the sermon is thorny—man must fight—but promises glory for the race as a whole. Underneath, however, slowly emerging, is his pseudo-Calvinist counterdynamic of election. The chosen individual and the overforce are brought into direct contact; the human center, the traditional arena of heroic action, vanishes. This Calvinist pattern, and its structural figure of ellipsis, represent, more than conscious design, a collective myth—and a national one perhaps, if we judge from the emergence of archetypes like Rip Van Winkle. The leap to Heinlein's big novel of the '60s, *Stranger in a Strange Land*, represents a *prise de conscience*. Clearly, here and in later works Heinlein becomes more and more aware of this underlying dynamic. He not only accepts it, but his experiments in form—more elaborate, self-conscious subversions of new and diverse traditional patterns—mark an attempt to enthrone it at the heart of his fictional world. It is not that these later novels are more didactic; they simply begin to teach his view of things more openly.

THE TWO SMITHS

Stranger in a Strange Land (1961) opens a new decade of Heinlein's fiction, and *I Will Fear No Evil* (1970) closes it. Superficially, the two novels resemble each other: both are inordinately long; their respective heroes are named Smith. What is more, they share the dual themes of religion and sex. Many have seen here a shift in orientation. With these 'bolder' themes a 'new' Heinlein was hailed by readers: this was proof that SF was at last becoming less parochial. In reality, however, religion and sex always lay beneath the surface of Heinlein's novels, even the most innocuous. They had simply been carried and buried by the conventions of adventure and intrigue. Now, as these conventions are subverted, these themes finally emerge. Heinlein is not wearing a new skin; the old one has merely been turned inside out.

And yet these two works are essentially very different. *Stranger* is a novel of religion, *I Will Fear No Evil* a novel of sex. The distinction is subtle but real: in the former, it is religion as sex, in the latter, sex as religion. With the name Smith, we expect a hero who is Everyman, and in both cases get superman. But again there is a fundamental difference: the protagonist of *Stranger* is young, that of *I Will Fear* old. There are twists, of course: the Martian Smith, it turns out, was an 'Old One' all along, while old Johann Sebastian Bach Smith (the name marks his antiquity) is rejuvenated in the most astounding manner. Yet the distinction stands, and points to an important development in Heinlein. *Stranger* may be an elaborate farewell to the world of the juvenile hero. But in *I Will Fear*; suddenly, we are in a twilight landscape—here is the most extreme decrepitude. The earlier novel promises adult preoccupations, adult responsibility. These never come to be—its hero is destined not for adulthood but sainthood. Between these poles of youth and age is ellipsis, the two Smiths staring at each other across a gulf. And yet the leap is made—Heinlein's novel of the '70s will be an excursion in the land of the walking dead.

The two years of silence between *Starship Troopers* and *Stranger* seem full of promise. But how new is the work that emerges? In sheer bulk, *Stranger* was the largest novel published by Heinlein to that time. It contains enough raw material for several novels. In its form, it is clearly a hybrid of the sort already studied, if extended on a much vaster scale. Like *Double Star*, it opens with the promise of political intrigue and adventure; once again, this initial thrust is redirected as the book unfolds. In the course of its development, it breaks into several disparate sections. Yet, in spite of the patchwork nature, the book has a certain unity. This can only be the product of a greater doctrinal purpose in *Stranger*. Various parts of the novel may have been written at different times, to different ends. But these strands, surprisingly, are woven into a framework of ideas which is coherent. At its root are the familiar patterns of election and providence. Not only are these obviously recognized and understood in *Stranger*; they function more openly as well. The religion set forth in this novel has praised for its 'purity'—here is something basic, unseen since the days of apostolic Christianity. Such Edenic interpretations are blindness. In *Stranger*, the only way to the Apostle lies through the impure bog of materialism and native Calvinism.

At the heart of this doctrinal web is Michael Valentine Smith—infant survivor of the first scientific expedition to Mars. Heinlein's space voyages are invariably promiscuous. Not content to send out shy gods to conquer, or to observe and legislate, he brings along the forces of fertility as well, to sink racial roots in new soil, to hold and exploit the land. Mike is born of two such elite pioneers. Indeed, this is fortunate promiscuity, for when the rest of the crew is decimated, one survives. This interplanetary foundling is raised by Martians—their culture and mental powers become his. Twenty-five years later a new ship goes to Mars, and brings this handsome young 'man' back to Earth. Smith, of course, is naive—a stranger in a strange land. He is also a prime political prize: as the sole survivor of his expedition, he inherits the 'rights' to Mars. In the first part of the novel, Smith's re-education is set aside. He is kidnapped by government agents, rescued from prison by Jill Boardman. She takes him to Jubal Harshaw; intrigue gives way to legal machinations. After incredible complexities, Harshaw secures Mike's freedom. The young person wanders in search of his being, discovers it, and finds a 'religious' vocation. This Martian-who-is-really-a-man combines the best of both worlds: man with his sexual potentiality, his dynamic incompleteness, learns to harness his powers by 'grokking' (establishing an immediate communion with another thing or mind). Mike's 'church' rapidly gains members, and begins to pose a real threat to the establishment. His enemies close in, a howling mob surrounding his headquarters. In Christ-like fashion he walks among them, to death and martyrdom.

Stranger combines the novel of political intrigue, the *Bildungsroman*, and something like a saint's life or narrative of martyrdom. In the progession of this omnibus work, from one stage to another, we have an extraordinary example of multiple ellipsis. Heinlein undermines his initial action plot by setting up contrapuntal lines of social satire of forensics—Smith in his new land, Harshaw in the courtroom. The possibility of individual heroism is given to secondary figures, Jill and Ben, who conveniently fade away as their actions are rendered inconsequential. But what is more interesting, the subsequent (and long delayed) novel of formation is subverted as well. In doing so, Heinlein, who has denied heroic action, now cancels the possibility of guided growth to adulthood as well. There will be neither earned glory nor earned responsibility. In the third section, we are left with two absolutes—Mike and Jubal, youth and age. This elaborate machinery leads to the apotheosis of this fundamental Heinleinian polarity.

In Heinlein's juvenile adventures, the pairing of boy and mentor is commonplace—it is the dynamic of innocence and experience. Often, at the end of the action, there are curious reversals. The boy, now seasoned, discovers his mentor is really his own 'dad'—the old lord will bend to the new. Or the mentor will marry the hero's sister, and thus place himself on an equal (if not inferior) place. Or he may go on a time voyage, and return younger than his charge. In our two 'subverted' novels, this relationship becomes most disquieting. Through the various twists of providence, concourse between these extemes becomes more direct, and even incestuous. The middle ground of adult maturity, through which common mortals pass, is elided. The Einsteinian equations will not allow Tom his adulthood. He returns to Earth, still young in the mirror of Pat's age, and a virtual innocent in this new world. Lorenzo slips painlessly from early manhood (with its attendant insecurities) to Bonforte's wise maturity. But he cannot remain there. His life must be spent in the domain of infirmity, impersonating a prematurely aged man. In both cases, the center is denied.

The relationship between these poles in *Stranger* has become oddly symbiotic. There is Jubal Harshaw, the old self-reliant man, seemingly full of wisdom. And there is young, vigorous Michael Smith. Harshaw speaks and acts with authority, as if he had nothing more to learn, and everything to teach. Indeed, he has had enough experiences and accomplishments to fill ten lifetimes. Could one so knowing ever have been young and foolish? In reality, his actions in the novel are supremely childish, mere displays of power and virtuosity for the sake of showing off. His old age is but an illusion; we are looking at the energies (and callowness) of extreme youth.

Smith, on the other hand, is not only young, but promises to grow up. During his *Lehrjahre*, as he moves from experience to experience, he is apparently being shaped, prepared for the ultimate revelation of self and mission in the adult world. All the mechanics of the *Bildungsroman* are present, but the whole process, we discover, is one monstrous tautology, a travesty of *Bildung*. Smith is, after all, human; he comes from Mars to learn what he was all along—a man. Experience does not lead to discovery of a new state of existence—it uncovers the old. What is more, beyond this point of 'recognition,' he is not permitted to develop either. Instead of adult leader of the faith, he becomes elder, then saint. Mike came from the Martian 'Old Ones' in the first place; now, in an instant, he returns to our heaven to sit among the patriarchs. The young man is never actually young. During his sojourn on Earth, he is a false youth, who overleaps the vale of tears to embrace an antiquity of spirit. Jubal and Mike are opposites only in a nominal and positional sense. Actually, each is a hermaphrodite—not in terms of sex, but of time. Each is both old and young. The process of reduction that runs through Heinlein's novels is nearing its end here. In a work like *Double Star*, what had seemed to be antithetical states are drawn into a relationship that is clearly polar. Now these poles have begun to blur, to melt into a single common point.

On the most rudimentary level, the components of Heinlein's 'new' novel are the stock ones. The secondary figures remain types. For example, though *Stranger* preaches love and union of free partners, its women are still essentially props. The trio of secretaries who surround Harshaw have as little individuality as the Misses Alpha, Beta and Gamma Furtney in *Time for the Stars*. In that novel, of course, triplets are even more interesting than twins, in terms of patterns of telepathic communication. If anything, the fact they are female, with unpredictable emotions, hinders the scientific experiments they participate in. Their names, however, compensate by making notation easier. These are guinea pigs; Heinlein intends his threesome in *Stranger* to be 'real' women—he gives them exotic names and even more exotic physiques. In spite of this, they remain the same faceless automata, varieties of sexual experience rather than persons.

Not all women in Heinlein are such. In many earlier novels, we find the Amazon figure: often she can out-hunt and out-fight the male protagonists, and seems ferociously independent of spirit. Yet inexplicably, in the presence of the hero, she succumbs to some mysterious power and authority. The domestic role she had eschewed before is assumed with astonishing ease. At the outset, Jill Boardman seems such a heroine. She is both more cunning and more effective than Ben Caxton. Nevertheless, she falls in with him. As the novel progresses, we see that Ben is not to be the 'magic one,' a role reserved for the man from Mars himself. The story shifts to Harshaw, then to Smith, and Jill's heroism must be submerged. As Mike draws her attention, she becomes first an experimental sex partner, then a high priestess in his faith. In Mike's harem, she discovers that she and another priestess, the dancer Dawn, look exactly alike. In Jill's case, the promise of individual heroism has been totally dissipated. Ultimately, she loses not only her autonomy, but her identity as well.

The other shadows who comprise Smith's 'inner circle' are equally stereotyped. Heinlein gives us no step-'n'-fetch-it Negroes this time, but more than compensates by tossing in outrageously caricatured Arabs and Jews. Mahmoud is both unctuous and sensuous (as well as a bit indolent). His nickname is 'Stinky,' as it is well-known that the Musulman shuns water. The Jew, Saul, is naturally a good businessman. Heinlein's racism is all the more insidious in that he preaches just the opposite of what he practices: Mike's message of love has broadened the racial base, broken down these artificial barriers, caused all these contending faiths to sit down at one common table. And yet these figures are hollow masks, mere ciphers. They then can offer no resistance, either as individuals or as representatives of individual religions, to Mike's centripedal pull. If rascism and holy wars must go, it is only because they are inefficient: they impede the advent of the true master.

Finally, there is Jubal Harshaw. He is not just a super-mentor—he represents a further development of a character type. The technological wizard has disappeared (Heinlein purposely makes him all thumbs when it comes to gadgets). Jubal is aloof; machines merely serve him; let lackeys build and service them. Nor is he the pure man of action either. Dak Broadbent was still lean and mean; Jubal (as his name tells us)

is a fat sybarite. His field of action is intellectual, his mode
defensive. Rather than fight intruders, he simply keeps them
out. In the past, he has been both a doctor and a lawyer; now he
writes trash fiction. But all this he does 'just in passing,' in
order to secure his independence from the world out there. Not
only does he have a unique life-style, but he has built a self-
sufficient community in its image to sustain and perpetuate it.
Harshaw, however, though intended to be the supreme individualist, is hardly an individual at all. Jill waxes, then
wanes; on a more grandiose scale, Jubal does the same. If his
isolated community dominates the first part of the novel, it is
later supplanted by Mike's universal institution. His maneuver-
ings and presence fill the early pages of the book; but as Mike's
influence grows, his contracts to a point. Far from maintaining
his independence and individuality, Harshaw is caught up in
what seems a predetermined rhythmic movement, a systolic
and diastolic pulsation. As a self-reliant ego incarnate, Jubal is
the center of *Stranger's* world, and Mike Smith and his religion
its circumference, its oversoul. The interaction of these two
poles, it seems, is the product of some higher destiny.

The first part of *Stranger* could stand as a Heinlein novel in
miniature. Indeed, Some critics believe he wrote this section
during the 1950's, laid it aside unfinished, then took his narrative up years later. Whatever the case, the initial intrigue and
political imbroglio is typical of any number of standard Heinlein
novels, from *Beyond this Horizon* (1942) to *The Puppet Masters*
(1955). Because of his legal status as 'owner' of Mars, Mike in
his innocence is beset by Earth's ruthless politicians. He is held
prisoner by the government in the hospital where he is supposedly under 'observation.' Ben Caxton, a newspaper man,
tries to penetrate the veil of secrecy surrounding the Man from
Mars, and is kidnapped. His girl friend, Jill Boardman, a
nurse in this same hospital, enters the action, abducts Smith,
and the chase is on. Jill is overtaken; Mike 'discorporates' a
couple of cops, then goes into suspended animation, and is
taken in a suitcase to Harshaw's Hideaway. As in the opening
pages of *Double Star*, we have all the makings of a good adven-

ture. And similarly, once the sanctuary is reached, things bog down and the action slows to a crawl. What is more, there is a sudden shift of focus, in the manner of Heinlein's 'subverted' novels. Suddenly, the center of attention is Jubal Harshaw: we study his way of living, listen to his brilliant analyses, observe his manipulations of the political machinery, and clap as he foils his opponents. Brute force and dumb cops are easily brushed aside. The climactic moment, characteristically, is a public assembly: Michael Smith appears before a new interplanetary assembly of nations; Harshaw's gambit wins Mike and Mars for the forces of justice. In this welter of protocol and legal subtlety, the initial intrigue is hopelessly lost.

Onto this trunk, Heinlein grafts several sections: there is a long series of episodes dealing with Mike's apprenticeship to life; digresssions on the Fosterite Church, where satire is mixed with an obvious fascination for the workings of this organization; and finally, a huge passage on Smith's own sect, where we are taken on guided tours, listening to endless discussions in which various matters of doctrine are exposed and refined. As a whole, this exemplary part of *Stranger* forms one of Heinlein's most colossal centerpieces. Waiting at the end of the tunnel, in all its anticlimactic glory, is Mike's death and transfiguration, that long-delayed return to action. Various strands of potential dramatic development from the fast-opening first section fall into and through this middle part, but do not completely disappear. The budding romance of Jill and Ben, for instance, is needed to get things rolling, but must necessarily fade away if Mike's world of communal sex and 'sharing' is to triumph. There is no place for the torments and struggles of orthodox romance. Jill and Ben, however, can serve other, more didactic purposes, and much later in the novel Heinlein resurrects them. Ben grows jealous of his old girl friend as she 'grows closer' to Mike. But this moves not into violence, but back into dialogue. Jubal takes Ben aside, and gives him a talking-to. The power of Mike's logic is such that Ben instantly sees the light, and becomes a convert. On the plane of ideas, jealousy has become a handy counterpoint, and monogamous love a potentially dangerous enemy, a doctrine to be refuted. The same thing happens with Duke's defection. Early in the book, he quarrels with Jubal over Mike. Xenophobic, he resents having a Martian around, especially one so apt at human ways of sex and seduction. Duke disappears; but fears that he was told the authorities of Mike's whereabouts lead to nothing. Duke shows up much later, a changed man; he even joins the new faith. We have no idea how this change comes about, or whether Duke has experienced much anguish of spirit. But is this not all the more proof of Mike's fabulous powers? If a dramatic point is lost, a doctrinal one is apparently made. For this potential Judas is left without even a kiss.

From the start, however, the actions of both Jill and Harshaw are undercut by what is essentially a 'Smith strand.' Throughout the novel runs a strong current of social satire. It begins with the arrival on Earth of the naive outsider. Heinlein uses an old device common to the satirists of the 18th century: Mike's 'innocence' is meant to expose, as in a mirror, the absurdities of a society supposedly civilized, but in reality barbarous and totally corrupt. Much of the best writing in *Stranger*, in fact, deals with the alien's encounters with the language and mores of Earth. These can be quite humorous. For example, Mike is asked: "Feel like breakfast?" and replies: "He knew that he was food, but did not 'feel like food.' Nor had he any warning that he might be selected for such an honor. He had not known that the food supply was such that it was necessary to reduce the corporate group." Beneath this whimsical surface, however, there are serious implications, which go much farther than a mere attack on our culture. For Smith, language is supposed to be the literal image of things; in our metaphorical minds, it has become a divided image, ultimately a means of duplicity; Smith, in spite of his misunderstanding, acts candidly nevertheless—though this custom seems odd to him, he "enfolds and praises" it. Are we meant to do the same with cannibalism— "a custom which Smith found proper?" On the surface, this may seem no more than a plea to open-mindedness: this could be a solution to the food problem, or at least teach us not to waste our resources. But there is more here than the lesson of relativity. Smith's vision is in its literalism (it is implied), the most 'truthful'—our linguistic habits themselves, in which words have become arbitrary signs, bearing no intrinsic relation to the things they name or recount, damn us. We have not progressed, but fallen away from primal unity.

We are meant to see the early Mike as a new Candide, who will go from experience to experience until the blank page fills. We have before us the example of some generally valid norm. But the expectation is misleading. From the start, Mike is neither innocent nor average. In fact, the 'basic' values he sets against our byzantine ways are rather ominous. Sex is a notable example. The Martian ignores it, even though he is eminently capable of it—his culture knows only 'water-brothers.' Mike, therefore (and Heinlein seems to relish the situation), must be taught, and by the numbers. But this goes beyond satirical commentary on man's artificial mores—it goes beyond voyeurism as well. Sex, Mike discovers, unleashes new powers of the self. The Martian learns to draw upon the dynamic instability of this basic human relationship. But he 'purifies' it, and in the process, harnesses and directs this new source of energy to his own ends—power and domination. This exemplary satire does not establish laws and limits: rather, it enthrones lawlessness. Smith, indifferent to all collective norms, will later protect certain individuals, and destroy others. Again the rationale is some 'purer' affinity, beyond analysis, and unassailable.

The purpose of satire in this novel is not to reduce excesses to a reasonable mean so much as to play one extreme against another, in order to push forward something even more outlandish. This is clearly seen in Heinlein's comparison of languages. Long passages of *Stranger* deal with the Martian language—it is supposedly the key to Mike's religion. The tongue is marvelously simple to those who 'grok' it: one need only converse in Martian, and relationships fall each in their 'proper' places. Heinlein sets the Martian tongue against the 'adspeak' of a not-too-distant American future, where poverty and injustice are concealed behind jingles of slogans. The spectacle of Mike's immolation (his followers watch it on television) is interrupted every ten minutes by ads for "Cahuenga Cave, the night club with real Los Angeles smog." Purposely, this future is made much like our present. We are meant to condemn our society, and to condone Mike's alternate vision—his 'real' language and 'selfless' deeds in place of our artifices and mass brutality. This is an insidious travesty of Christ's passion, and the openness of the New Testament. The Martian tongue is not at all universally accessible; in fact, it poses an insurmountable barrier to all but the fortunate few who possess some mysterious insight into its workings. Nor is this language as 'innocent' as we are led to believe: apparently, it is even more an instrument of power and exclusion than society's slogans—visibly and tangibly so. When Mike 'groks wrongness' in someone, he need think no further. In Martian, the map is the territory—he 'discorporates' his adversaries (kills them), with scarcely the bat of an eye.

Much of the satire in the latter two thirds of *Stranger* is directed at the Fosterites. Heinlein's portrait of this mercantilistic sect of the future is thoroughly amusing. For them, the temple and market-place are one: when a follower strikes a jackpot on the slot machines in the vestibule of their tabernacle, he gets 'Three Holy Eyes.' Sex and sacrament have become indistinguishable. One of Heinlein's characters, Patty Paiwonski, the tattooed lady, cherishes most, among her markings the indelible imprint of 'Foster's Holy Kiss' on her breast. True, the Fosterites are descendents of today's bible-waving zealots. Heinlein captures their unctuous rhetoric, exposing the hypocrisy and venality of their faith in their rhythms of speech. Once again, we are intended to contrast such crass displays with Mike's message and creed, which claim to eschew material possessions for universal loving-kindness. But there is more to the Fosterite episode than simply knocking over another straw man. Heinlein is clearly fascinated with the organization of this sect. The tone, instead of being satirical, is ambiguous. As he attacks it, Heinlein describes the methodology of this 'church' in the most intricate detail. Indeed, as Mike's cult develops, we see just how indebted to Foster's church it really is. At the very least, Jubal tells us, the Fosterites eschew cruelty and whimsical tyranny—here is a well-managed purveyor of earthly delights, something far more sensible than its superstitious precursors. The mystique of the 'New Revelation,' of Foster in Heaven, is a necessary concession to the masses. To Jubal's sharp eye, however, it conceals a very worldly power structure, aimed primarily at profit. This is clearly a step in the right direction. Mike opposes this episcopal structure with his doctrine of individual freedom of choice. Yet, as we shall see, his followers are also selected—and by an order far more inscrutable and absolute than Foster's deacons. Mike eschews 'possession' and ownership in all forms. Yet his disciples, inspired by more than mere earthly appetites, dream of clandestine control of the world, and in the process become a band of super capitalists.

In the final sections of *Stranger*, all pretense at satire is dropped. Instead, we have two sorts of moot dialogue. In the first, Harshaw confronts a series of puppet interlocutors; in the second, Jubal and Mike interact, and the ultimate doctrinal configurations are played out in a highly stylized fashion. The purpose of the Harshaw dialogues is to expound Mike's new religious 'philosophy'; makeshift stumbling blocks to its comprehension appear, only to be swept aside by the master dialectician. The second series polishes and refines these principles. They are, in fact, less didactic than illustrative, in a quite literal sense. Only on the surface is this a classic exchange between teacher and pupil. One figure does not alter the other so much as both adhere to each other—in Martian, it would be called 'growing closer.' If we expect to see at this crucial moment individual destinies being shaped and separated, each going its different way, we are doomed to disappointment. Instead, these opposites merge, forming complementary parts of the same body. The form that emerges is not the representative of mankind so much as its epitome, less a shape than a dynamic rhythm, a creative polarity. It defies death, overcoming the limits of the individual body. Mike's spirit comes back to dwell in Jubal, to purge him of the poison he has taken, and save him from his own death. By doing so, this last and toughest individualist is fused with Mike's universal order—center and circumference now coexit and coincide.

An example of these dialogues is the scene with Ben, who visits Mike's temple to see how things are run, but finds himself unable to participate. Ben's crisis is not narrated directly as a dramatic scene. We hear of it second hand, as he tells Jubal of his experiences. Ben is unable to diagnose his malady; Harshaw cross-examines him, uncovering the roots of jealousy: Ben still wants Jill for himself. Poor Ben's individual problem is raised to exemplary status: such possessiveness is, of course, the chief enemy to Mike's gospel. Each man carries the seed of destruction in his own mind, but can purge it if he erects a Jubal-like conscience. Harshaw may seem out of place preaching against egotism. But we are intended to see him as self-reliant rather than self-centered. Jubal is master of himself, and thus free to choose or not to choose. Ben is still a slave to passions and possessions. Harshaw may hold back from Mike's collectivity at this point, but at least he understands it. Jealousy, however, is simply incomprehensible.

Such is the doctrine Heinlein purports to teach. Smith claims his new faith is a matter of free individual choice: the way to god is through personal effort, and responsibility to self. The facts, however, belie these statements. In reality, Smith's religion is not open to just any man who can master its discipline; only the predestined few can participate. These elect are somehow seized, often unbidden, by some irresistible force. Duke and Ben, for example, though initially opposed to the faith, are converted in a flash, and yield without the least bit of struggle. Neither man has done anything to make himself worthy of this honor. No matter, they are 'first-called' among the original 'water-bearers;' their election remains fundamentally unearned. Indeed, Jubal is prime proof that deeds have nothing to do with being chosen. Mike tells us his religion is one of works and individual accomplishment: learning Martian is the key to salvation. Many struggle and master the letter, only to be ultimately denied the spirit. Jubal, however, though he steadfastly refuses to learn Mike's language, is nonetheless elevated to the inner circle. The many aspirants are denied entry not on any rational, objective ground, but because they cannot 'grok.' This is some form of intuition, or inner light. Either a person has it intrinsically, or never will, and all the good deeds and hard effort in the world do not seem to help.

Out of the original dispensation, a new elite descends. Only one who 'groks' can know his brethern, and recognize the mark of election. These few sit at the doors of the temple, and decide who will enter and who will not—their decision is absolute and beyond repeal. Typically, the original circle is chosen in heaven, subsequent apostles being named by these 'first called', and so on—the dynasty is established. Heinlein's new religion is archly Puritanical. True, the sexual license, body painting, and togetherness orgies seem strange garbs for fundamentalist religion. But Heinlein shows that the two are not incompatible. If we see only pagan rejoicing in the body, or rejection of artificial strictures in favor of nature, we are wrong. These things are opiates, and, when ultimately spread to all humanity (as Mike wishes), will serve to enforce barriers further. The Fosterites have their slot-machines, Christianity its promise of an afterlife. Mike offers sex without fear, but also without the responsibility of continuing attachments. Rather than a vision of heaven on earth, this is actually an open admission that the world is hopelessly fallen. Depraved man remains isolated in his flesh, unable to rebuild through will and effort new structures to replace the old. The elect may preach their doctrine of free sex to the *hoi polloi,* but they rarely practice it themselves. We see very little sensuality for its own sake in the inner circle. Though tolerant in minor matters, this society is actually quide rigid and hierarchial. Table conversation turns invariably to matters of power and domination. What sex there is seems to be aimed at breeding new saints. Like many other closed groups in Heinlein, this one gradually degenerates into a vital statistics column.

Another Puritanical pattern can be observed here. While

works are not sufficient for election, election does lead to works, or efficient action. Mike stresses, in fact, what is basically a work ethic: "You see, Jubal, it's not a faith; the discipline is simply a method of efficient functioning in anything." The relationship he draws between election and material success is familiar. If one is elected, he necessarily succeeds; thus, if one succeeds, he is obviously one of the elect. Mike's vision finds its analogue, its double, in the Social Darwinism espoused by Harshaw. The fittest survive, and in so doing are elected according to nature's laws. The best men will always be there to carry the race forward. In the final pages of the book, Mike despairs because the majority of men will not heed him. Harshaw consoles him with these words: "If one-tenth-of-one-percent of the population is capable of getting the news, then all you have to do is show them—and in a matter of some generations the stupid ones will die out and those with your discipline will inherit the earth." In this dialogue, nature, tooth and claw, and Mike's messianic prophecy, are no longer contradictory. They have become complementary, forming a closed, self-modifying system. Harshaw's initial view is grim, but it still offers freedom of action, if only within the narrow limits of competitiveness. Mike, however, even though he speaks of glory, closes the door: man survives not through deeds, but through his predisposition to grace. Now, in his final words, Harshaw has corrected his vision: it is receptivity, 'getting the news,' that counts above all.

Just as Harshaw's natural 'philosophy' is rectified and balanced by Mike's more metaphysical insight, so also is the interaction of these two set in yet a larger framework. *Stranger* contains a number of scenes in 'Heaven.' Linked with this cosmic framework is a higher spy plot. Mike learns halfway through the book that he has been sent to Earth by the Martians on a reconnaissance mission, to gather information about man and his civilization. The 'Old Ones' of Mars must decide whether mankind will be allowed to survive. Here we return to a theme that is found often in Heinlein's novels: did the Martians destroy the mythical fifth planet, and the advanced culture which presumably inhabited it? Will they now do the same to Earth?

'Heaven' in the novel is the comic, Byronic variety. The presences are presented as petty bureaucrats. Here as elsewhere, of course, Heinlein would celebrate man, and the destiny that drives men to advance their race. What is interesting is that the angels are only paper-pushers, scribes for some greater, invisible power. Moreover, their actions on Earth are apparently part of some vast (and possibly unfathomable) plan. The founding of the Fosterites seems as much a part of this design as Mike's mission, since Foster too is an Archangel. Mike is a tool of the Martian 'Old Ones'; but in the last scene in heaven, he appears as the Archangel Michael. In some vague sense, all these Old Ones, Martian or Terran, are linked in a mighty web. What seems opposition, is in reality a kind of polar rhythm. Smith is nowhere a stranger, nor are Earth and Mars strange lands.

Heinlein erects his machinery, and we are left to ask why. If the goal of this 'plan' is to glorify mankind, as Heinlein insists, then how will this be so? Heinlein's view of Mars has been surprisingly consistent throughout his long career. Even in the early juvenile *Red Planet* (1949), Mars is an old culture, far superior in knowledge and wisdom to Earth, yet decadent, no longer a vital, dynamic race. The Martians tolerate the human presence on Mars largely from inertia; wrapt in their own preoccupations, they pay little attention to man, as long as he behaves himself. But when human greed and folly overstep their limits, the Martians are goaded to act. Several times men on Mars have come close to being wiped out *en masse*. The Martians of *Stranger* are cast in this same mold. The expedition of Mike's parents caught their attention, and now they are pondering man's collective fate. They have two options: colonize Earth, or destroy it. They have no intention of doing the former: it is human stupidity to try remaking another race into one's own image. While man's existence is no menace to the Martians, they might destroy him on esthetic grounds, because his existence offends their sense of beauty. It is this solution they are apparently pondering in their tranquillity.

In the meantime, however, mankind is progressing. Michael Smith, Martian by culture, discovers the grandeur of being hu-an. Through his erotic experiments, Mike supposedly discovers a deep truth: ours is a dynamic race precisely because we have two sexes. Men and women must not be seen only as anti-thetical beings, but rather as polar opposites, always striving to reunite and coalesce. Thus, where Martians can only 'grow together' symbolically, man does so literally. Instead of mere-ly 'sharing water,' he shares a physical person. Basically, Heinlein's Martians are Platonists—they prefer shadows to material reality. What Mike discovers is that physical contact a-lone generates the energy of life. Mike also learns that not all men and women are capable of this dynamic union. The major-ity of humans are hopelessly divided within themselves; the spirit wars with the flesh. They can never hope to achieve their creative polarity; they remain eternally fallen. The fate of man-kind is in the hands of those fortunate few who have the gift. It is interesting that although Mike makes his discovery by meditating on heterosexual union, he himself is never able to find a woman partner worthy of him.

The true polarity in *Stranger* lies between Mike and Harshaw. In the culminating dialogue of the novel, Smith's idealism is apparently corrected by the practical vision of his mentor, redirected into action. The young man must reject Mars com-pletely. Jubal abhors this world, for it is the exact opposite of all that is human. It looks backward, not forward; things are run, not by the living, but by a horde of ancestral ghosts. Even the process of natural selection on Mars is backward: the help-less young are exposed to evolutionary pressures, while the old are artificially preserved. The emphasis of this culture is on fossil wisdom. Man, of course, protects his young, and lets adults fend for themselves—the process of competition gener-ates vital, progressive energy. Our 'Old Ones' also have the good sense to withdraw to their insignificant comic Heaven when their work is done. Harshaw pushes the religious prophet in the direction of decisive action: "If you've got the truth, you

can demonstrate it. Talking doesn't prove it. *Show* people."
So Mike immolates himself, and in doing so rejects once and for
all the Martian principle, 'waiting is.' The way is thus cleared
for more dynamic things to come. Lorenzo's old maxim is lav-
ishly illustrated here: the show must go on. The goal of this process is revealed through an epilogue in Heaven: while the Martians continue to wait and ponder, man will push forward to the
point where he exceeds his enemy, becoming the destroyer in
turn.

Again this seems a general message of hope. But, as it turns
out, this destiny will not be for all men, but only for the chosen
few. What is more, for all the talk of decisive human actions—
deeds by which man moves forward to ultimate victory over impossible odds—we are shown none. On the contrary, Heinlein
repeatedly leaps over this heroic middle. All the key actions
are elided; things appear to change, but actually do not,
appear to move forward, but actually strike a static balance.
Significantly, Mike's martyrdom is not experienced first-hand:
we watch it on television. And, although he is brutally torn to
pieces in front of a world-wide audience, his death is only tem-
orary: he soon returns in spirit to his disciples, and is more
alive than ever before. Harshaw's attempted suicide is also
nullified. After he takes an overdose of sleeping pills, Mike's
spirit enters and purges him. Not only are actions powerless to
change the course of destiny, but that destiny is more fortunate
than anyone could have imagined. Indeed, the climactic ellipsis is the final leap to Heaven. With Mike dead and reborn, we
have the promise. And suddenly, there is the answer: man will
overcome. This time, predestination itself is made manifest—
we see the outcome simultaneously with the beginning.

All dramatic possibilities in *Stranger* contract to polarity.
Stranger does not go forward; it undulates between poles that
are fixed and deathless: Harshaw and Mike, Earth and Heaven.
These terms shrink even further as the book develops; opposition itself is an illusion. The process of self-discovery does not
come (as Heinlein would have us believe) from man's relation
with the external world, but rather with himself alone. Emerson

says: "He who knows that power is inborn, that he is weak because he has looked for good out of him and elsewhere, and, so perceiving, throws himself unhesitatingly on his thought, instantly rights himself...commands his limbs, works miracles." And Michael Smith echoes this: "No matter what I said they insisted on thinking of God as something outside themselves." Smith himself experiences such a 'perception,' and in a flash the elaborate pretense of *Bildung* vanishes. His epiphany comes as he watches the antics of man's ancestor, the monkey, in a zoo. When he enters the zoo he is still a stranger, separated from mankind by the mystery of laughter. Intuitively, he laughs; he realizes that he is a man, and that man is God. Supposedly, laughter is man's heroic response to a tragic existence. Smith, however, has experienced neither tragedy nor heroism. In fact, his instant discovery of the God within obviates the necessity of a tragic journey without. In this moment of ellipsis, the Martian is suddenly a man, the callow boy a God. Circumference and center themselves coincide and become one. Mike all along was both Martian and human. His credo turns out to be that of the immortal Archangels—"Thou art God," the crowning contraction. In transitional novels like *Time for the Stars*, young and old become doubles. In this new book, they are openly one. Not only does Mike attain instant wisdom, but in the end he has become, and has always been, both young and old simultaneously—the boyish Archangel Michael. Harshaw too is not only resurrected but rejuvenated. the attempted suicide is prompted by the burdens of age: his hour is past. Inhabited by the youthful spirit of Mike, the old man awakens to a new dawn.

Emerson speaks of 'power.' Mike also derives force to 'work miracles' from his revelation. He does so, however, in a very special sense. After his central illumination, he gazes out over the sleeping city: "There is no *need* for them to be so unhappy." But this is not an expression of universal compassion—it is a declaration of power: I have the force to change things. Emerson's power is at least nominally spiritual; Mike's is blatantly material, and aggressively destructive: his only miracle is to 'discorporate' bodies that stand in his way. His creed is not universal but aristocratic, not charitable but arbitrarily exclusive and cruelly exploitative. He can preach freedom, and at the same moment divide the world with a wave of the hand into 'marks' and masters. All but his circle of elect are slaves—the iron bands that hold them are two: Harshaw's evolutionary vision is reinforced and sanctioned by Calvinist predestination. Man's wit can never triumph over nature in this bleak world, for nature is irremediably fallen. As Jubal sees it, man is powerless to change his lot: "Do-gooding is like treating hemophiliacs—the real cure is to let hemophiliacs bleed to death...before they breed more hemophiliacs." Ironically (and this is the last, most gruesome ellipsis of all), the masters too are not free of this fallen world. In spite of all the exhortations, progress in the sense of amelioration never occurs in Heinlein's universe. The elect may not have to suffer. But they are powerless to do more than generate more suffering, or to revel in it. Power in this world is a negative freedom at best.

I Will Fear No Evil (1970) has been promoted as a second 'cult' novel. Possibly, it was written in hopes of capitalizing on the somewhat belated success of *Stranger* in the late 1960's. While it appears to deal with the same themes as the earlier novel, beneath this surface is a work that looks in quite different directions. The book is inordinately long, much longer in fact than *Stranger*. And yet, paradoxically, *I Will Fear* marks a return to the simpler fictional structures of Heinlein's early career. Indeed, this top-heavy monstrosity is built around a single incident. There is a thin story line, and expanding out from it in vertical layers a profusion of illustrative episodes. The message is hardly worthy of even the most rudimentary of Heinlein's early stories. It is a thoroughly regressive work.

I Will Fear marks the triumph of a new figure: the hero as old man. The heroes of Heinlein's early adventure novels were either adolescents or, as in *Beyond This Horizon* and *Double Star*, young men.

Throughout the 1960's, however, from Harshaw and Hugh Farnham to the hero of this novel, Heinlein's leading characters gradually become older. Johann Sebastian Bach Smith is, in fact, at the extreme limit of physical existence. As Heinlein himself ages, it seems, the problems of old age, the possibilities of prepetuating the individual, of immortality in the flesh, come to dominate his fiction. *I Will Fear No Evil* then, is perhaps best seen as Heinlein's first large-scale attempt to create fictional forms that can accomodate this preoccupation. In the sense, the novel is transistional, leading directly to the author's most recent work, *Time Enough for Love.*

If *Stranger* is a patchwork of many diverse elements, *I Will Fear* is an overly long novel in which a single element is stretched to the breaking point. Its actual 'plot,' once all the accretions are pared away, is hardly more substantial than that of the early Heinlein story it most resembles, "Requiem" (1940). In "Requiem," Heinlein tells the story of Delos D. Harriman, the Lunar entrepreneur who never made his trip to the Moon. Harriman is now an old man; to undertake the trip at this point is suicide. But the Moon is the only dream he has left, so he charters a ship, travels there, and dies a happy man. Heinlein uses a simple story to demonstrate a simple human truth.

Johann Smith has also reached the end of his life. He like Harriman is rich. What he decides to do, however, is quite different—he has his brain transplanted into another body. The operation is successful, but Smith awakens to find himself in the body of Eunice, his beautiful secretary, who had conveniently died as he went under the knife. Smith's plan (once the shock of discovery abates) is to impregnate this body with his own sperm, which he had deposited earlier in a sperm bank perhaps out of clairvoyance. Life on Earth has degenerated beyond recall. He will fly this new seed, mankind's hope, to the Moon. This is the plot—uninspired Heinlein—and it predictably comes to be. The huge center of the novel is given over to the vagaries of this odd co-habitation. The man must get used to being a 'woman.' He must also make peace with his secret sharer. For some unexplained reason, Eunice's 'spirit' continues to haunt its old body. Her 'mind' and Smith's are locked in the same skull. Heinlein spins out infinite variations on these perplexing problems.

Various themes and motifs from *Stranger* undergo an interesting change here. *I Will Fear No Evil* has vaguely the same social framework as the earlier book—a dystopian urban America of the near future. It is, however, far more ominous. The world of the streets is an anarchic jungle, with lawless roving bands and ubiquitous murder and violence. But evidently, the fittest do not survive by fighting so much as by withdrawing. The hero lives in fortress isolation—here is an island of total freedom in the midst of groveling necessity. How is this obtained? Smith reminds us of Jubal Harshaw. He possesses great resources and infinite wisdom; he has amassed a stupendous fortune. We do not, however, learn how he got all this. We do not even see him in action. How Harshaw developed his talents was a mystery, but he did have ample opportunity to display them. Smith can only belabor us with drab tales of clever schemes. We are several times removed from the realm of heroic deeds and individual formation. Smith's powers are simply given; he is chosen to conduct, in perfect security, the bizarre experiments that (as Heinlein tells us) will carry mankind forward. The only ones who count in the world of *I Will Fear* are Smith's entourage. This handful of the elect have everything within their grasp effortlessly. The rest of humanity is consigned without recall to their hell on Earth.

Often, in this novel, the reader has no idea where he is going. There are scenes of social satire—Heinlein lambastes the linguistic and moral hypocrisy of this brave new world—but they seem gratuitous, not subordinated to a general frame of ideas, as were the Fosterite episodes in *Stranger*. Both Smith and Jake Solomon (a lawyer, naturally) have Harshaw's ability to manipulate. But there is nothing really to manipulate in this novel. In *Stranger*, there was the issue of Mike's legal status: the ownership of Mars was at least an international issue, requiring a grandiose trial scene. Heinlein tries to drum up the same kind of interest here, but the issue is dull and petty. Smith's brain transfer also creates a legal problem: is this the same 'man?' If not, his relatives inherit his fortune. These human vultures swoop down, to have him declared legally dead. In earlier stories—*The Star Beast* (1954) is an example—Heinlein created lively court scenes, full of witty forensics. Here we see an endless series of dreary legal technicalities. Most of the action, in fact, takes place behind the scenes, in the judge's chambers. Indeed, most of the important matters are treated there. The focus inexplicably shifts: the outcome of the trial (we learn) was never in doubt. The real issue is Johann/Eunice's sexual flexibility. This is tested as the androgyne proceeds to lay the various lawyers (who are both homo-and heterosexual) one by one.

Now familiar patterns—the indestructibility of the elect, their hermaphroditic tendency to fuse in one body—are bloated to insane proportions. Chronicling this process of absorbtion, in labyrinthine detail, becomes the central concern of Heinlein's novel. Smith not only gets Eunice's body, he gets her 'spirit' as well, which apparently abides as long as it has a material home to dwell in. Primarily, though, Eunice is a voice, and a talkative one: we listen to their endless conversations inside one common skull. Heinlein's two-headed mutant Joe-Jim, in *Orphans in the Sky*, is perhaps a prototype. This earlier creation, however, is far more dramatic, for the contending heads could at least nod or bump each other. In the Johann-Eunice dialogues, on the other hand, we frequently lose our bearings, and cannot tell who is talking. To compound matters, a third sharer arrives. Jake Solomon dies late in the novel, only to be resurrected inside this overcrowded head. Now two bodiless men (one of them Eunice's physical lover, the other her mental lover) cling to a woman's body as it ripens with the impossible seed that is meant to prolong them all. The baby will need a central switchboard to control all of this 'racial memory' or run the risk of drowning in gibberish.

Michael Smith 'discorporates'; Johann Smith literally 'incorporates' all around him. The process is not a spiritual one at all: it is crassly materialistic. Everything outside Smith's household can go to hell; everything inside must be physically absorbed. As the hero sets out to lay everyone around him, he is not uniting so much as enslaving—this family of love is more a prison than anything else. Starting with the doctors who performed the operation, Johann-Eunice subdues all in turn, including the lawyers and judges associated with the interminable court proceedings. He/she then seduces the ageing superstud, Jake, and finally starts working on servants of both sexes. Heinlein's publishers have called this risque; actually, it is quite orthodox, if one considers that the hero is both male and female. It is not homosexuality so much as pansexuality. Even more bizarre is the voyeuristic delight Heinlein seems to take in narrating certain situations. The hero will be loving a man, for instance, while the Johann persona looks on, making wry comments, and providing helpful hints. If this is sexual deviancy, it is by proxy only. The vicarious nature of these scenes betrays their author's Puritanism, as does their total lack of humor. In the hands of someone else, this situation might have provided endless opportunity for comedy. Here it is painfully boring.

Sex dominates this book. And yet it remains superfluous to its central concern, just as the anarchy in the streets is. Heinlein creates another 'nest' where no one need worry about money or other contingent factors, and where people can spend all their time and energy 'growing closer.' But no sooner do things contract to this point than they begin to expand again. Onanistic fantasy gives way to something much different (if no less ambiguous). The 'action' of *I Will Fear* covers exactly a year. During that short time, however, bellies are already swelling, and random impregnation is rampant in Smith's colony (none of Heinlein's characters ever mention birth control; no doubt it infringes upon their 'freedom'). But all of this is irrelevant. As the fling goes obsessively on, and the narrator tallies his vital statistics, Johann's baby is inexorably coming to term. This is the only one that counts. In the end, all these insubstantial beings, will fade before the hard realities of genetic selection, and man's destiny in the stars. Does it matter what the other bellies contain? This baby, Johann's creation, is the predestined one.

Johann's struggles seem an odd sort of exemplum. Heinlein does proclaim the old faith in man and science. And it is true that science gets this baby on the Moon. But how incredibly complex and tortuous the process is! For the first time, perhaps, Heinlein's simplistic view of predestination meets genuine opposition. Compared with the cosmic sweep of *Stranger*, this novel is narrow and confined. There are no scenes in heaven, or visions of immortality; there is only a decrepit old man who goes to unbelieveable pains to buy an extra year of life. Is the title of this work an affirmation, a statement of faith in election? With the first three words, however, the accent is on fear. Indeed, a plan does work out unexpectedly here; but, we are far from the easy 'serendipity' of *Time for the Stars*. Anxiety is now one of its prime movers. In *I Will Fear*, Heinlein taps a deeper Calvinistic current: election seems uncertain; death as the moment of truth is something to be feared. Perhaps Johann is one of the elect; but why does he seek so frantically to avoid his destiny?

Behind Johann's anxiety lies a peculiarly materialistic tenacity. In this novel, 'souls' cleave to the flesh at all costs, individual egos strive to preserve themselves *this* side of paradise. Actually, what we have here are not souls but material spirits, vaporized egos, dependent on a body for existence. Johann marshalls the formidable apparatus of modern science to give himself a strange kind of 'immortality': instead of spiritual peace, he gains only more time and space. Why did he not simply have children when he was younger, and thus prolong his line? Evidently, he wants more, and a bizarre stroke of luck brings it to him. The male role is easily replaced by a sperm bank. But, by actually becoming the woman who bears his seed, he moves physically closer to the being who must succeed him. Through such contiguity the material spirit will perhaps abide. If predestination is at work here, its ways are astoundingly tortuous. Heinlein seems to amend Whitman's line: "*Not* to die is different from what anyone supposed, and luckier." And yet luck is muted by grisly irony: Johann runs from the fate of all flesh only to be plunged more frantically into

48

the flesh. Prisoner of the quantitative, he undergoes torments
akin to Poe's fear of premature burial. The spirit dreads living
on to witness the corruption of the flesh, and yet the uncertain-
ty of blackness (where even nothingness is more merciful than
the possibility of judgment) drives it to raise the corpse, returning to physical life in any form and at all costs. In *I Will Fear No
Evil*, the old romance motif of the child of promise—of renun-
ciation of self in order to forward the destiny of the race—is
perverted into a bizarre form of recycling. Johann-Eunice
dies in childbirth, and his/her son lives on.

THE DEIFICATION OF LAZARUS LONG

Time Enough for Love (1973) is an immense novel built
around one man, Lazarus Long, Senior of the Howard Families.
In his many 'lives' and incarnations, Lazarus is the hero of this
vast *roman-a-tiroirs*. *Time* returns to the world of Heinlein's
earliest fiction. *Methuselah's Children* (1958), to which this
book is nominally the sequel, lies at the center of a cycle of stories intended to depict the 'Future History' of human civilization. Heinlein reorganized this Balzacian epic in his recent col-
lection, *The Past Through Tomorrow* (1967), which includes the
famous chart of names, places, and events prominent in his
imaginary scheme. *Time Enough* is presented as the capstone of this Future History. Not surprisingly, many characters
from earlier works make new (if brief) appearances here. Johann Smith's brain transplant is even mentioned in passing,
although *I Will Fear* is not formally part of this saga. Apparently Heinlein would tell us that all his novels are 'history' in this
same sense. Indeed, each of his stories can, if necessary, be
classified according to the names and dates on the master chart.
Obviously, Heinlein intends Lazarus, whose existence spans the
entire period, to be both center and circumference of this
mighty fictional structure.

Like *Stranger*, Heinlein's latest novel makes extensive use of
forms and devices borrowed from the didactic fiction of the
eighteenth century. Again, the exemplary thrust is elided.
The novel is fashioned of diaries, inserted documents, sayings,

and aphorisms; there are even footnotes, and an 'editor' who supposedly has rearranged all the miscellaneous materials into unified form. Each of the tales is intended to illustrate some aspect of Long's exemplary life. There is, however, only a semblance of progression. The novel does not narrate his becoming so much as celebrate his being. Overriding these linear expectations is a 'musical' structure which is openly circular. Chapter headings announce "Variations on a Theme," or "Counterpoint." The final story of Lazarus' return to the Earth of his past is titled "Da Capo." This novel, Heinlein is telling us, has fugal form. In essence, there will be different temporal and spatial arrangements of a single basic theme—diversity in unity. In terms of progression, the work inscribes a circle: in the end, we return to the beginning. All possibility of heroic action is gone forever. Even the polar dynamic has given way to open exaltation of the singular. There is one hero, one theme, and one world—and all these are one: Lazarus Long. It is a novel of solipsism.

At first glance, Heinlein may seem to be redecorating old material with a profusion of structural novelties. Not only is *Time Enough* well crafted, but its ambitions are vast and well-executed. Heinlein would do nothing less than merge the two axes of his fictional universe. Lazarus's life covers the whole range of his adventure tales, and absorbs them all. In the vertical sense, he subsumes all other exemplary figures in Heinlein. *Time*, in fact, is intended to be a truly philosophical novel. As far as the destiny of mankind is concerned, it begins not *in medias res*, but at the end. An ancient Lazarus ponders Hamlet's dilemma: to be or not to be. This old man has not only done everything there is to do, but through his 'family,' he has brought civilization to a state where even the 'evil' of death is no more. But if death was a quandary for Smith, the possiblity of endless life is one for Lazarus. The hero of *Methuselah's Children* struggled to survive, and the challenge gave value to his life. Now, however, with nothing left to accomplish, no adventures to be had, Lazarus wonders (and all mankind with him) what he has to live for. He faces a new, and more insidious enemy—boredom.

Stranger elides the tragic possibilities of death. If it occurs at all, it becomes, in the larger perspective of human destiny, merely another step on the way, not a harrowing finality. *Time Enough* begins beyond death. Man's science has now defeated Johann Smith's enemy. The human race, in fact, has entered a utopian phase. Along with death, it seems, man has done away with the need for God: the idea of immortality in Heaven has simply become irrelevant. Michael Smith's gospel was: "Thou art God"; Lazarus, however, now discovers the danger in being a god. To replace destiny is to become static; on the contrary, man thrives only in a dynamic situation. The old hero of *Methuselah's Children*, who rejected paradise in favor of struggle and the unknown, is still alive in this new world at the end of time.

All decisions have apparently been made: man has reached a state of rest. Evolution has abolished the heroic world, and, it seems, has broken the Calvinistic hegemony as well. Not only has man conquered death, but he himself forsees and arranges all 'surprises' now. Lazarus's actions will prove, however, that man has not reached his destiny. Heinlein's latest novel does not suspend the Calvinistic pattern, but reaffirms it. In this static world, Lazarus has apparently found the one choice that remains: to die. But his situation is falsely existential. As it turns out, he does not choose, but is 'tricked' into continuing his existence. And this is a most fortunate occurrence, for Lazarus's ensuing experiments, his search for a *raison d'etre*, lead the intrepid voyager to new, unheard-of discoveries. If man's possibilities again prove unlimited, it is clear that this man of action also does not guide, but is being guided. Science may aid Lazarus in his new search. Yet without this initial 'grace,' man's efforts will invariably flounder. The proof lies in the book's initial situation: man masters the physical universe, only to find himself faced with even graver problems—matters (in Lazarus's words) of a 'spiritual' nature. Once more, the course of this novel is governed by 'serendipity.' Heinlein may want us to exclaim: "a mighty maze, but not without a plan!" Lazarus's journey back from utopia, if anything, reverses these terms. Even more than for Johann Smith, the plan leads Heinlein's hero into a nightmarish maze. Long's quest to relieve spiritual anxieties only takes him deeper and deeper into the prison of matter; in his search to expand man's horizons, he loses himself in the labyrinth of his own personality.

Time Enough For Love advances on two parallel levels: the past world of Lazarus's adventures, and the present one of metaphysical boredom. In the latter, Heinlein describes a "sensually polymorphous" culture in which Lazarus is a "living fossil." The exotic and erotic world of Ishtar and Galahad (the 'bed-names' of two of his descendants) is static. Age is now mainly a cosmetic problem. In direct contradiction to Michael Smith's philosophy, gender is now considered unimportant in sexual relationships: indeed, Ishtar is surprised (pleasantly) when her partner for "seven hours of ecstasy" turns out to be male. Reproduction is under perfect genetic control, and has become an 'art.' The sex change of *I Will Fear* is mentioned in passing as something utterly barbaric. Such matters are now routinely accomplished through cloning. Genetic engineering will allow Long to make his first experiments in life beyond death.

Paradoxically, however, the direction Lazarus takes is not (as we might expect) expansive, but contractive. The title of the novel presents two terms: time and love. Its grammatical logic relates them not in linear but in polar fashion: they are rhythmically dependent on each other. Lazarus has all the time he wants. We would hope to see a new center, love, expanding to fill this periphery of time, thus giving value and meaning to what otherwise is a material void. Just the opposite happens, however. As the novel progresses, Lazrus gradually draws the external world completely into himself. If this is love, it is solely of self. In turn, expansion from this center seeks to people time and space with more images of the self. As ancestor of the Howard Families, Lazarus is the seed from which this world has sprung. In the various action tales, we watch him as, step by step, he shapes it throughout history. Now he would give it a soul, a basic rhythm at its heart. What we have, instead, is Narcissus and his mirror.

Long's taste for life is restored at first by the possibility of rectifying certain errors of time. Men can be rejuvenated indefinitly, but no one can completely turn back the clock. Lazarus is offered a way to fill in an important gap. Through cloning, he can now have the sisters he never had. The twins that result are, paradoxically, both sister and daughter. The cloned cells are implanted in host mothers, Ishtar and Hamadryad, both of whom are Long's mistresses. Johann Smith, through luck, became a woman, and thus was able to bear his own child. Long does not need to do this. These children have no biological contact with women at all: the role of mother has been subverted to that of carrier. And yet these outward forms are scrupulously maintained. Love-making here is divorced from conception, and even becomes a travesty of it. These children are genetically identical with the hero; they *are* Lazarus. Nevertheless, he goes through all the forms of being father to himself. In a sense, he must, for the biological processes demand that this prolongation of self be carried and raised as a daughter. Within the recurring rhythms of life, the same individual reproduces himself endlessly.

Because everyone is related to Lazarus in some way or other, incest is a constant danger in his world. Or perhaps, in the manner of Heinlein's fortunate paradoxes, it is a blessing. Heinlein cultivates these paradoxes on both levels of narration. In one of the inserted tales, Lazarus tells of the "twins who weren't." These creatures are 'diploid complements,' products of genetic manipulation. Long rescues them from a circus freak show, and takes them into space. Again, we have a Heinlein novel in miniature. Following this active beginning, we bog down in technicalities. These healthy adolescents are ignorant of the 'facts of life,' and all in love with each other. Many pages are devoted to Lazarus's proving that these 'facts'are wrong: they can indeed marry and have offspring. In fact, he shows (with interminable statistics) that Joe is really the *best* possible mate for his sister. Wonders never cease. Even more astonishing is Lazarus's parallel love-making with his own sister-daughters. This time it is his turn to be convinced by irrefutable logic: "We are artifical constructs, and the *soi-disant* 'incest' mores of another time and utterly different circumstances don't apply to us...that's just an excuse to avoid something you don't want to do. Coupling with us might be masturbation, but it can't be incest, because we aren't your sisters. We aren't even your kin in any normal sense; we're you. Every gene of us comes from you." Here is an odd variation on the Pygmalion myth—the ideal woman turns out to be another form of the creator himself—and a strangely solipsistic mode of masturbation. The inspiration only appears to be another; it is really the self.

In the *da capo* episodes, Heinlein explores the ultimate form of incest—love of mother. Long journeys back in time to the place of his origin. As a mature man (he has undergone rejuvenation), he faces himself as a small boy, and sees his mother as a possible lover. Another ersatz family is formed—an ideal that can never be, but is miraculously realized in the flesh. Son and father stare at each other as mirror images. The time shift has, simultaneously, created this pair of doubles, and also the conditions which will break them apart. In their ensuing rivalry for the mother's affections, the two men fight over the source of their own life. In this scene, Heinlein perfects the art of titillation. Will Lazarus seduce his mother and conceive himself? This cannot be—Lazarus is already born, and the mother is pregnant with another: here is double protection against contamination from the future. In spite of this, however, the drama of seduction is elaborately acted out. The mother falls in love, and would have Lazarus at exactly the same spot, and in the same clothes and position that she had used that wild night years before when she had conceived him. This re-enactment, happily, is thwarted *in extremis* by none other than Lazarus himself—the little pest has sneaked a ride in his mother's car. Is Heinlein parodying his own doctrine of predestination here? We seem to be closing the circle, but at the last minute, good luck twists things, and we have a spiral. Here, as in all the other episodes, incest only appears to stifle—

in stranger and stranger ways, the dynamic of the universe still carries things forward. The ultimate Heinleinian paradox is this: man can lose himself in contemplation of his own image, and yet be part of a vital ongoing dynamic.

The drama in these scenes is contrived. The reader is titillated by the possibility of disaster, only to be pulled back in time. The inserted tales are of the same sort. Here, however, it is Long himself who plays destiny. The stories both illustrate his talents for manipulation, and give him the opportunity to voice his wisdom. In the diploid twins episode, for example, Llita is made pregnant by her brother, and Lazarus deploys a fantastic array of intellectual fireworks to resolve this seemingly impossible situation. In fact, the only intrigue we have in this scene is his logical advance: step by step, we breathlessly await the result. The crisis over, another immediately arises: now the twin's own children have grown up, and want to marry each other, just like Mom and Dad. Once again Lazarus comes to the rescue. He gives a lesson: "Starting cold on the complexities of genetics with persons who don't even know elementary biology is like trying to explain multidimensional matrix algebra to someone who has to take his shoes off to count above ten." The specialist is needed to resolve situations only the specialist can dream of. Lazarus, of course, manages; the youngsters pair off, in genetically acceptable fashion.

More than ever, Heinlein seems to take a prurient delight in all these proceedings. He appears to savor the scientific lectures on the facts of life (why else dwell ad nauseum on such banalities?). Through the eyes of Lazarus, he looks tenderly on as sexual matches are made between diverse adolescents in the name of technology or family integrity. And there are always ready-made families on hand to work with. For example, the problem of incipient incest arises a second time, mirror fashion, in the pioneering episode with Lazarus and his 'ephemeral' beloved Dora. The family is isolated, and the sexual awakening of the adolescents poses a danger to the group. Needless to say, Long steps in with diversionary games (idle hands are the devil's play), until real help arrives in the form of another big family. Then the matchmaking begins in earnest.

Time Enough for Love is more than a sequel to *Methuselah's Children*; it reaches across the span of Heinlein's career to answer questions left unanswered in this earlier novel. In *Methuselah*, the Howard Families flee Earth to escape persecution: their longevity makes them the object of envy among more ephemeral mankind. They land on the Elysian world of the Little People. Eldorado, however, is not for man; the Family begins to stagnate there for lack of challenge and adversity. Lazarus rallies those settlers whose wills have not been permanently crippled, and takes them back to Earth. Once again, relativity and luck save the day. When these voyagers get home, they find that Earth scientists (inspired by the colonists' example) have discovered a means of extending life. Ironically, this new development creates a situation much like that on the Elysian planet: longevity brings widespread conservatism and fear of change. These, along with overpopulation, mark the decline of Earth's civilization. There is no promised land, apparently, for this new Moses and his chosen people: Lazarus must again head for the stars.

In *Time Enough*, the Elysian world of the earlier book has become universal. Ironically, it is man's very strivings and refusals that have ultimately brought him to this impasse once again. This time, however, the circle seems air-tight. Action and adventure are things of history and memory. Lazarus' one pleasure lies in recollecting his past. In his story of the trek over Hopeless Pass, he dwells lovingly on the long list of articles (now all obsolete) he needed for survival. His latest homestead on 'Boondock' has been designed to resemble a Pompeiian villa, complete with elaborate Roman baths. The past has now become merely a lifeless decoration, an artifice at the service of ever more sophisticated eroticism. What does a man like Lazarus have to live for in such a world?

In *Methuselah's Children*, Mary Sperling, faced with a similar dilemma, defected to the Little People. Lazarus now recalls the incident with horror: rejuvenation was not unlimited at that time, and Mary had succumbed to the onslaughts of old age.

Her attraction to the Little People was understandable. In their way, they had conquered death; the individual was absorbed into a collective consciousness that transcended the limits of any one body. Any such dissolution of self in the totality of man is anathema to Lazarus. His view (strongly tainted by the Calvinist doctrine of election) is radically different: not only is the individual spirit inviolate, but so is the body itself. Indeed, the spirit is not the issue here. Mary keeps her spiritual integrity; Lazarus can still talk to a 'Mary Sperling,' and receive an answer. The odious thing is that she must share her body with every other mind; the shell has become no more than a walking zombie.

Lazarus' actions in *Time Enough for Love* constitute a protracted answer to Mary's actions. She had chosen out of fear, and had thrown away her very self. Lazarus claims to act out of 'love,' and apotheosizes the self, expanding it to embrace and absorb that collective periphery Mary and the Little People had occupied. Lazarus becomes the world, quite literally. With each new act of love, he subdues a more recalcitrant pocket of resistance, reduces another duality to that unity which is himself. His multitudinous incarnations throughout history, and his prolific family life, make him the fountainhead of mankind. Now he lives to tighten the bonds between himself and his offspring even more. These bonds are always physical: bodies cloned from his are rejoined to it through fornication. The impossible barriers of time and space are neatly elided as Lazarus carries on his affair with his mother. Michael Smith made great promises for copulation. Now, in the person of Lazarus Long, it becomes the act through which space and time are physically conquered. Mary Sperling's denial of self was hardly altruistic. Lazarus's love requires no giving at all, except to self.

Heinlein has much to say about love in this book. One statement made by Maureen comes to the heart of the matter: "She liked herself...and liking yourself was the necessary first step toward loving other people." In reality, it is the all-consuming step. Lazarus's constant concern for his myriad families, his patriarchal complex, his fascination with mirror twins and doubles, his obsession with incest—all are manifestations of an all-devouring solipsism. All the women Lazarus loves are either created or recreated in an image he alone provides. The most interesting example if that of Minerva, the computer-become-woman. As Long tells the computer the story of his love for Dora Brandon, an 'ephemeral,' Minerva falls in love with him. The computer can have such human yearnings (we are told) because man has made it in his own image—the machine becomes but another face in this gallery of fictional mirrors. The only thing denied it is Eros. To feel lust, the machine must become flesh and blood. Minerva chooses this option, and abandons a timeless world for one which, in comparison, is quite ephemeral. Thus, in a reverse sense, she takes the same step Dora did when she married Lazarus centuries earlier: eternity and transcience are drawn to the center point which is Lazarus Long. The ties between Minerva and Dora run deeper still. In the course of a chance conversation, the computer asks Lazarus to describe what he would like 'her' to look like if 'she' should become a woman. The portrait he gives is that of Dora. When Minerva finally steps forth in human form, his description has been brought to life: Dora is reborn in Minerva's most unusual 'flesh.' And when these two make love, time and space are literally abolished. It is more than serendipity. In becoming 'Dora,' the machine has conformed absolutely to the wishes of Lazarus. In a sense, then, 'she' too becomes but another projection of Long's ever-present self.

Heinlein carries this theme to even greater heights. The most recalcitrant antitheses are abolished. With his cloned sisters, the lover can play both roles at once: "If we love you—and we do—and if you love us—and you do, some, in your own chinchy and cautious fashion—it's Narcissus loving himself. But this time, if you could only see it, that Narcissist love could be consummated." Lazarus's adventures with his mother destroy further barriers in time as well as space. In coupling with her, he joins himself to the very same life force which originally produced him. Heinlein stops short of having Lazarus actually father himself: the first cause must remain both inviolate and mysterious, an inimitable act of grace. But, by linking with the same force that bore him, he physically encompasses everything in between. In his greatest understatement, he says: "I'm a solipsist at heart." The full significance of this confession is revealed on the last page of the book. Lazarus seems to have met his end at last on this battlefield of the past. But the time paradox is, of course, on his side: he cannot be here when he belongs there. We learn, however, that there is another reason for his indestructibility: he belongs everywhere. He awakens to the sound of a 'Gray Voice': "You are you, playing chess with yourself, and again you have checkmated yourself."

Lazarus's initial question, "Why should man live?" is answered with a tautology: "living is." All of history, drawn to this point which is Lazarus Long, becomes one huge *carpe diem*: "Life is too long when one is not enjoying now. You recall when I was not and wished to terminate it. Your skill—and trickery, my darling—changed that and again I savor now. But perhaps I never told you that I approached even my first rejuvenation with misgiving, afraid that it would make my body young without making my spirit young again—and don't bother to tell me that 'spirit' is a null-word; I know that it is undefinable...but it means something to me." In spite of this declaration of faith, 'spirit' remains a 'null word' here. Lazarus's universe consists of a first cause—that moment of grace out of which the chosen company of Howard's evolve—and an ongoing, seemingly open-ended dynamic. The only soul in this machine (we are told) is human intelligence itself, and it is shaped in the processes of natural selection, led onward by recurring strokes of good fortune. These have, by now, come to be as predictable and mechanical as Heinlein's 'evolution' itself. We expect Lazarus to be 'tricked;' we expect paradox to save the day. The world of *Time Enough* is one of endless matter, of quantity and extension. Long's spirit is not elevated, it is rejuvenated. Love does not transcend this world; on the contrary, it becomes the means of reducing all things to one point. Basically, this novel offers the same message as *Stranger*: "thou art god." When he hears the 'Gray Voice,' Lazarus thinks for a moment that it might be God; he asks to see its face, and is told: "Try a mirror." But if there is no God; there is no 'other' here either—only an all-loving Lazarus staring at himself. The only double the hero has, apparently, is the author looking back at him. Lazarus's Missouri childhood has obvious autobiographical overtones. The deification of Lazarus Long must be, without a doubt, Heinlein's consummate solipsism.

There remains, nevertheless, a 'Gray Voice,' and it is more than Lazarus simply talking to himself. Brooding over the destiny of the hero is the familiar Calvinist theology. It informs the mystery that surrounds Lazarus's origins. He was born a normal man, in a world where scientific breeding and rejuvenation techniques did not exist. Why then has he lived so long? His life is a puzzle that even the most advanced genetics of the future cannot answer. The only solution to this enigma is grace: at this arbitrary point in time and space, some power enters the biological processes of nature, and the Howard Families are born. If there is a plan, its contours lie beyond human logic and reason.

But if Lazaraus is the first cause, what is the final cause, the end of this destiny? For Long, the end is death; and he, unlike Johann Smith, appears ready to meet it. However, the structural rhythms of *Time Enough* tell us quite the opposite. Lazarus assures us that he fears no evil; the entire novel is shaped around rejection of the valley of shadow. Ironically, horror of the unknown has led Heinlein to create an even more terrifying eternity this side of the tomb. The 'Gray Voice' may tell Lazarus: "There is no time, there is no space. What was, is, and ever will be." Actually, there is nothing but time and space in his universe: Lazarus lives on to twist and turn forever in these infernal circles and spirals. The hero's name is itself most significant: intended, perhaps, as ironic defiance. The name in Hebrew means 'God has helped,' and Lazarus has indeed proved that he alone is God. The name merely marks off the appalling limits of Long's universe. *I Will Fear No Evil* was a novel about raising the dead. Science may have advanced far beyond Dr. Frankenstein, but the results of Smith's experiment remain the same—he is still a monster. The Biblical Lazarus comes back to life in the flesh; the miracle of restoration is meant to prefigure the far greater one of resurrection of the spirit. Heinlein's 'Voice,' in proclaiming to his Lazarus, "You cannot die," dooms him at the same time to remain forever, on Earth or in the stars, a walking corpse.

Heinlein's latest novel leaves no doubt as to the frightful extent of his materialism. His anxiety is not (to use Baudelaire's expression) that man may never get free of this world of things and numbers; rather, that he might escape too soon, meeting in death a maker whose chosen being he may not be at all. In avoiding the chance of some unknown Hell, Heinlein's hero plunges into a Dantesque nightmare of his own making. Long before him, another man of science, Blaise Pascal, saw the danger in this position: "Physical science will not console me for the ignorance of morality in the time of affliction." Lazarus faces problems of a 'moral' order: man's position in the universe and his inadequacies. But this brave hero is at heart a moral coward. If Lazarus quests, it is not for spiritual finality, but for material exotica: he becomes a connoisseur of more and more involuted excuses not to die. Johann Smith's 'affliction' was physical; Lazarus's claims to be metaphysical. And yet the answers that come back to console him are invariably materialistic: more stars, more time, more love that is merely onanistic sex. But can an inexhaustible string of planets console even one man's anxiety? It was Emerson who saw that travelling solves nothing: man carries his problems with him wherever he goes. Ironically, as Lazarus expands, his human limitations only expand with him.

Once again, there is a surface and an undercurrent. On the face of things, Heinlein extols Lazarus's glorious destiny, preaching serendipity and the fortunate paradox. This time, however, the facade cannot conceal the much grimmer Calvinist patterns at work. In spite of the surface optimism, Lazarus's fate is a clear sign. In seeking to pre-empt destiny, the human intellect only falls further, dividing things even more. This hero reduces divisions only by isolating himself; in his ultimate solipsism, Lazarus comes to occupy the position of Lucifer himself. Heinlein clearly did not intend this to be. In a sense, though the author himself has undergone an analagous fall. *Time Enough* is a novel about an old hero, written by an old man. In it we witness the dissolution of the materialist creed before the onslaught of age and death. The only response to mortality has become a more and more frenzied cleaving to the body. This may throw new light on Heinlein lurking behind the endless sermons on freedom, there seems to be a fear that his heroes are really slaves; and behind the obsession with election, a fear that they are really damned. Heinlein is and always has been beset by Calvinist trepidations. This latest novel only reveals to what degrees the prophet of optimism and self-reliance has been, all along, a stranger in his own land.

AFTERWORD

Robert Heinlein may write more novels. However, it is safe to assume that, whatever their form, they will be little different in purpose and design from *Time Enough for Love*. All the earlier modes and forms are summed up in its dense texture; they, along with Heinlein's hero, have grown irrevocably old. Taking this work as capstone, his vast production may be studied and assessed as a whole. In discussing Heinlein's achievement, Scholes and Rabkin, in their recent study *Science Fiction: History, Science, Vision*, put the emphasis elsewhere than on literary excellence: "Students of American culture and values will do well to consider [Heinlein], for his contradictions and confusions are very much our own—as is his energy and the optimism that lies below his 'neo-pessimistic' facade." I have tried to examine Heinlein in this perspective. In light of the persistent Romantic and Calvinist undercurrents in his work, however, this description must be qualified. If there is optimism, it is for the elect only; for the common mass of men, there was never any hope, biologically or spiritually. And even for the chosen few, there is, in his latest novels, an increasing fear of death and an unwillingness to expose this unique individuality to what may lie beyond. The dynamic existence they substitute is merely an empty whirl of molecules. What characterizes a work like *Time Enough* (and all Heinlein novels to one degree or another) is a 'neo-optimism.' Beneath the facade of energy and purpose—which Heinlein must touch up more and more with fabulous feats of science and fantastic paradoxes—lies a realm of soulless perpetual motion. Heinlein's true land is materialist America. Out of its hopes and fears, he has fashioned, perhaps without knowing it, a new circle in hell.

* * * * *

Dr. Slusser discusses Heinlein's classic tales of science fiction adventure in his new book, *The Classic Years of Robert A. Heinlein*, available from the Borgo Press in October, 1977.

BIOGRAPHY

ROBERT ANSON HEINLEIN was born July 7, 1907, at Butler, Missouri, the son of Rex Ivar and Bam (Lyle) Heinlein. After graduating from the U.S. Naval Academy at Annapolis in 1919, he served in the Navy until receiving a disability discharge in the 1930's. His first professional story, "Life-Line," appeared in the August, 1939 issue of *Astounding*. Heinlein married Virginia Gerstenfeld in 1948. He is the only man ever to win four Hugo Awards for best SF novel of the year (for *Double Star, Starship Troopers, Stranger in a Strange Land,* and *The Moon Is a Harsh Mistress*). He was also the first recipient of the Nebula Grandmaster Award. His papers and correspondence have been collected by the University of California, Santa Cruz.

BIBLIOGRAPHY

Rocket Ship Galileo. Charles Scribner's Sons, New York, 1947, 212p, Cloth, Novel.

Space Cadet. Charles Scribner's Sons, New York, 1948, 242p, Cloth, Novel.

Beyond This Horizon. Fantasy Press, Reading, 1948, 242p, Cloth, Novel.

Red Planet. Charles Scribner's Sons, New York, 1949, 211p, Cloth, Novel.

Sixth Column. Gnome Press, New York, 1949, 256p, Cloth, Novel.

. reprinted as: *The Day After Tomorrow*. Signet, New York, 1951, 160p, Paper, Novel.

Waldo; and, Magic Inc. Doubleday, Garden City, 1950, 219p, Cloth, Coll.

. reprinted as: *Waldo: Genius in Orbit*. Avon, New York, 1958, 191p, Paper, Coll.

The Man Who Sold the Moon. Shasta, Chicago, 1950, 288p, Cloth, Coll.

Farmer in the Sky. Charles Scribner's Sons, New York, 1950, 216p, Cloth, Novel.

Between Planets. Charles Scribner's Sons, New York, 1951, 222p, Cloth, Novel.

. *The Green Hills of Earth*. Shasta, Chicago, 1951, 256p, Cloth, Coll.

. *Universe*. Dell, New York, 1951, 64p, Paper, Novella.

A. expanded as: *Orphans of the Sky*. Victor Gollancz, London, 1963, 160p, Cloth, Novel.

. *The Puppet Masters*. Doubleday, Garden City, 1951, 219p, Cloth, Novel.

. *Tomorrow, the Stars*. Doubleday, Garden City, 1952, 249p, Cloth, Anth.

4. *The Rolling Stones*. Charles Scribner's Sons, New York, 1952, 276p, Cloth, Novel.

4A. reprinted as: *Space Family Stone*. Victor Gollancz, London, 1969, 267p, Cloth, Novel.

5. *Starman Jones*. Charles Scribner's Sons, New York, 1953, 305p, Cloth, Novel.

6. *Revolt in 2100*. Shasta, Chicago, 1953, 317p, Cloth, Coll.

7. *Assignment in Eternity*. Fantasy Press, Reading, 1953, 256p, Cloth, Coll.

7A. reprinted in abridged form as: *Lost Legacy*. Digit, London, 1960, 156p, Paper, Coll.

8. *The Star Beast*. Charles Scribner's Sons, New York, 1954, 282p, Cloth, Novel.

9. *Tunnel in the Sky*. Charles Scribner's Sons, New York, 1955, 273p, Cloth, Novel.

20. *Double Star*. Doubleday, Garden City, 1956, 186p, Cloth, Nov
21. *Time for the Stars*. Charles Scribner's Sons, New York, 195
    244p, Cloth, Novel.
22. *The Door into Summer*. Doubleday, Garden City, 1957, 188
    Cloth, Novel.
23. *Citizen of the Galaxy*. Charles Scribner's Sons, New York, 195
    302p, Cloth, Novel.
24. *Methuselah's Children*. Gnome Press, Hicksville, 1958, 188
    Cloth, Novel.
25. *Have Space Suit—Will Travel*. Charles Scribner's Sons, New Yor
    1958, 276p, Cloth, Novel.
26. *Starship Troopers*. G.P. Putnam's Sons, New York, 1959, 309
    Cloth, Novel.
27. *The Menace from Earth*. Gnome Press, Hicksville, 1959, 255
    Cloth, Coll.
28. *The Unpleasant Profession of Jonathan Hoag*. Gnome Pres
    Hicksville, 1959, 256p, Cloth, Coll.
28A. reprinted as: *6 x H*. Pyramid, New York, 1961, 191p, Paper, Co
29. *Stranger in a Strange Land*. G.P. Putnam's Sons, New York, 196
    408p, Cloth, Novel.
30. *Podkayne of Mars, Her Life and Times*. G.P. Putnam's Sons, Ne
    York, 1963, 191p, Cloth, Novel.
31. *Glory Road*. G.P. Putnam's Sons, New York, 1963, 288p, Cloth
    Novel.
32. *Farnham's Freehold*. G.P. Putnam's Sons, New York, 1964, 315p
    Cloth, Novel.
33. *Three by Heinlein* (includes *The Puppet Masters*, *Waldo*, an
    Magic, Inc.). Doubleday, Garden City, 1965, 426p, Cloth, Col
33A. reprinted as: *A Heinlein Triad*. Victor Gollancz, London, 1966
    426p, Cloth, Coll.
34. *The Moon Is a Harsh Mistress*. G.P. Putnam's Sons, New York
    1966, 383p, Cloth, Novel.
35. *A Robert Heinlein Omnibus* (includes *Beyond This Horizon*, *The
    Man Who Sold the Moon*, and *The Green Hills of Earth*). Sidg
    wick & Jackson, London, 1966, 644p, Cloth, Coll.
36. *The Worlds of Robert A. Heinlein*. Ace, New York, 1966, 189p
    Paper, Coll.
37. *The Past Through Tomorrow*. G.P. Putnam's Sons, New York,
    1967, 667p, Cloth, Coll.
38. *I Will Fear No Evil*. G.P. Putnam's Sons, New York, 1970, 401p,
    Cloth, Novel.
39. *The Best of Robert Heinlein*. Sidgwick & Jackson, London, 1973,
    348p, Cloth, Coll.
40. *Time Enough for Love*. G.P. Putnam's Sons, New York, 1973,
    605p, Cloth, Novel.